DISH

Rhys Nicholson is a multi-award winning Australian comedian, writer, actor and presenter. Alongside a booming live and televised stand-up career – with performances in Australia, New Zealand, the UK and North America, and on Netflix – they are a favourite across our small screens too, from panel shows to documentary, acting roles (in the sci-fi comedy *The Imperfects*) and as a judge on *RuPaul's Drag Race Down Under*. Hailed as 'an astute satirist . . . clever and blatantly very funny' by the *Sydney Morning Herald*, and 'hilarious and uproariously catty' by the *Herald Sun*, Rhys has opened for Conan O'Brien as he toured Australia, and is co-founder of Melbourne live comedy venue, Comedy Republic.

DISH

RHYS NICHOLSON

VIKING
an imprint of
PENGUIN BOOKS

VIKING

UK | USA | Canada | Ireland | Australia
India | New Zealand | South Africa | China

Viking is part of the Penguin Random House group of companies whose addresses can be found at global.penguinrandomhouse.com.

First published by Viking, 2023

Cover design by Alex Ross Creative and Rhys Nicholson
© Penguin Random House Australia Pty Ltd
Cover photography by Julian Kingma
Spoon image used on cover and internally by ery muhyiddin / Alamy Stock Vector
Typeset in 12/19 pt Adobe Garamond Pro by Post Pre-Press

Printed and bound in Australia by Griffin Press, an accredited
ISO AS/NZ 14001 Environmental Management Systems printer.

A catalogue record for this book is available from the National Library of Australia

ISBN 978 1 76104 675 9

penguin.com.au

We at Penguin Random House Australia acknowledge that Aboriginal and Torres Strait Islander peoples are the first storytellers and Traditional Custodians of the land on which we live and work. We honour Aboriginal and Torres Strait Islander peoples' continuous connection to Country, waters, skies and communities. We celebrate Aboriginal and Torres Strait Islander stories, traditions and living cultures; and we pay our respects to Elders past and present.

For my Granny, Nancy.

Granny, please, *please* do not read this book.

'My best hostess tip is to have good food and really good music.'

— Jennifer Aniston

CONTENTS

A LETTER TO THE PUBLISHER

A while ago the idea was floated that maybe I might like to try and write a book. I had a meeting with the nice people at Penguin Random House and it was decided I would write a little tiny something about what this book could possibly be. This is what I sent.

Dear Ms Penguin Random House,

Like most gay people in their late early-thirties, I've been groundlessly calling myself a writer for the better part of a decade. I mean, who's to say I'm not? I have opinions. I earn my living by performing live and haven't written a single book in more than thirty years. On those facts alone it could be argued I'm this generation's Fran Lebowitz.

But now, as I approach my early mid-thirties, I think it's

time I put your money where my mouth is. I would very much like to write a book, please.

For as far back as I can remember I've dreamt about being able to tell people 'I'm working on a book'. Let me be clear, the dream is not to write a book. Good lord, let's not get ahead of ourselves. Just to be able to mention I'm working on one. You see, I've yearned for the day I can be in a conversation with a complete stranger or my father-in-law and with a loud thud drop such phrases as, 'Well in the book I'm writing . . .' or 'I'm actually working on a chapter of my book at the moment about . . .' or 'Can you read? No? Oh, that's sad. I must send you a copy of my book when it's finished and maybe someone will read it to you.'

I am someone with no physical strength or any useful real-world skills. As a result, these small, beautiful moments of self-satisfaction I get from talking about my work are very important to me. I reckon I could safely say about 60 per cent or more of my waking life is spent telling people my intentions with absolutely zero plan of following them through. This is because I work in the arts. It's kind of our whole thing.

Now, what would my book be about? Well, I'm not a huge reader, to be honest. I get my fill of all that from street signs, social media and warning labels on unprescribed medications. Here are a few things I've jotted down: I had this idea for a sexy thriller novel about a Harvard professor leaping around Europe with a female companion solving murders by decoding ancient cryptic puzzles, but it was unfortunately recently broken to me someone has beaten me to the punch on that one. Then I thought there might be something in hiding an anti-trans allegory into a book series about a school for wizardry? No? What if I penned an autobiography of my tortured experience being a member of the British royal family?

I think it's for the best I just do a book of funny-ish stories and essays. Yeah? Because obviously that's what the world needs right now. As society and the planet burn, this ill-informed, opinionated homo wants to lecture the flames away with a negative attitude and a saucy turn of phrase.

You might be thinking a book of essays is perhaps a little basic and not enough of an idea. You'd be right. A little rude, but right. So, pondering on this notion I believe there could be something in the fact that I love to cook and I love to eat. And without looking into it too much, I think I'm the first person ever to say that, let alone deem it an interesting topic for a book. More than cooking and eating, what I love most is the act of talking about cooking and eating. I love having people over to our house with drinks on arrival as I tell them about the overpriced piece of meat I've bought from our young, inner-city pansexual butcher. I love to say, 'Excuse me, you guys keep chatting – I just have to check the oven.' I love to throw around words like 'brining' and 'bordelaise' and 'yeast'. I'm a real douchebag about it. Am I an incredible cook? Absolutely not. I'm not all that gifted at anything, really. If I were a contestant on one of those cooking competition reality shows, I'd have the vibe of a fifty-year-old divorced man who comes in confidently because he owns a barbecue. The one who fucks up a savoury tart and has to leave in the first week. The one who gets huge sweat stains on his polo shirt as he fights back tears because he's been beaten by mere pastry and eggs that somehow represent his relationship with his kids. Yeah, that's about where I sit mental-health wise.

Speaking bluntly, I'm sick of this stand-up comedy bullshit. There's only so much curly fries and house white wine you can consume at the back of comedy club. I just want an *in* to the part of show business that's all about food. That upper echelon, bougie class of TV personality whose whole deal is swanning around and eating nice stuff in pretty places. Not the type who actually has to make anything, *absolutely* not. Fuck that. Just the eating and the pretty places bit. Please, help me, you're my only hope.

Lastly, Ms Penguin, and I truly mean this with all of my heart, I feel I should point out that I know I can do this because I will approach it the way I have approached all my successful endeavours: spite. I'm riddled with it. Absolutely up to pussy's bow with contempt for my enemies and those who have wronged me in some way. Any way at all. I will work hard on this project because I need my high school bully, *NAME REDACTED*, to see it. Even though I haven't seen him in the better part of two decades. I need him to see this book. It's important that while he's on his lunch break from the job that he only got because his uncle owns the business, he's trudging past a bookstore and sees my face on the cover in the New and Noteworthy stand. He must see it and stop. Take it in. As he stands and stares at it, he should know deep in his gut that my life is better than his.

Regards,

Rhys Nicholson Esquire

LIFE'S WORK

When I was about eleven, my dad told me what remains my favourite old 'joke' joke. It's one of those with heaps of variations, but it essentially goes:

> A backpacker is travelling around Scotland and finds himself in a small, local pub sitting at the bar having a pint. Next to him is this grizzled-looking elderly guy. The old man slams his hand down on the bar and says, 'See this bar?! I built this bar. I went out to the forest, searched for the perfect tree, chopped it down and slaved for days. Lathing and sanding to make this bar for this goddamn town. But do they call me McGregor the bar maker? No.' He then points out the window and slightly louder exclaims, 'And you see that wall out there?! I built that wall. Broke every stone and placed them all by myself throughout this godforsaken country's brutal winter – wind, rain and frost. But do they call me McGregor the wall builder? No.' The backpacker tries to change the subject. 'Look, I'm just

here for a dri—' McGregor interrupts, essentially screaming at this point: 'And you see that pier out there? I built that goddamn pier. Collected the wood from that same goddamn forest. Drove the pilings against the tide, plank by plank. The salt water stinging my splintered, blistered, bleeding hands. But do they call me McGregor the pier builder? No!' There's a pause and McGregor leans in close to the backpacker and sighs. 'But you fuck one pig.'

At the time I laughed the way any eleven-year-old does when an adult has purposefully said 'fuck' in front of them. Now as a grown-up I see how perfect and relatable the moral of this joke is. I mean, we're all McGregor. Everyone's just out here trying their best to not be remembered by their peers for having full penetrative intercourse with a farm animal. Both metaphorically and, for a special few cases, literally.

Not everyone will admit it, but we all want a legacy. Right? It doesn't need to be huge. Just a little something-something that can be rattled off at a memorial. A moment or two from our life that's worth mentioning. But the big question is, *how*? How will you be recalled? What memory lane will you live down? There are myriad ways to go about making sure you're remembered. Some people do it by spending their entire lives striving to make a difference and creating a better world through sheer hard work. That's their legacy. But then some people marry their adoptive daughters and flee to Europe to make perpetually shittier movies. It's dealer's choice, I suppose.

Some of my favourite types of people are the ones who say they don't care about what others think of them. Sure mate, sure. They say things like, 'I'm just running my own race,' or 'I move to the beat of my own drum.' This is of course bullshit and the exact thing someone says if they are desperate for you to like them. It seems insane to me not to care what others think. It's human instinct. We all want to be liked and remembered fondly. Every single one of us. Even the most humble monk living up on some mountain somewhere hopes that the local villagers say something nice about him after he dies. 'I mean, look, the guy didn't say much and let's be honest, his religious views were pretty wild, but I think we can all agree that stew he made last harvest festival was absolutely off the fucking charts.'

One aspect of legacy that has always fascinated me is keeping a diary. The entire concept of which is lost on me. It's not that I have anything against it. Not at all. In fact, I have plenty of friends who swear by it. Many, many times I've loved reading the published diaries of influential people – David Sedaris, Fran Lebowitz, Schapelle Corby. All my idols. I just can't get my head around writing down all of *my* thoughts and opinions without some second party offering me a little pile of cash to do so. (Thank you, Penguin Random House.) For me, it feels as if I'm thinking to myself, *My god, my life is so deeply fascinating right now. I'd better write some of this shit down before I forget. I am a gift!* When I've tried it I can't help but find myself daydreaming about the life my words will have once I am long dead and buried. There's this fantasy we all have about journals where years after you die, some cluey great-niece of yours in a fun outfit finds your diaries in an attic and uses them to solve a massive family secret to uncover a huge inheritance and save the town's orphanage for unwed rescue dogs. Or some shit like that. The problem being, the handful of times I've given it a whack I always end up panicking, realise how dull my day-to-day is and just flat-out begin making things up. Tell you what, it's a very special mix of self-loathing and narcissism that leads to openly deceiving a book only you intend to read.

The main issue lies, I believe, in one blunt fact. You aren't interesting. I'm sorry. You're not. I mean, neither am I. Most people aren't. In all of history I reckon we can safely say there have only been about twelve or thirteen genuinely interesting people. And that's being pretty generous. Then everyone else we think is interesting is only considered interesting because someone once saw them standing next to one of the actually interesting people. The real kicker is that these truly interesting people have no clue how interesting they are because they're far too busy doing interesting things. That's the curse of being interesting. The exact moment you suspect you might be interesting, you cease to be.

Like McGregor, some people's whole identity is going to be tied to just one event. A singular action that sets up the way people will talk about them for generations. Bestiality aside, the roughest of these trots must be for those who are only remembered for the way they stopped living. Imagine, your entire life being simmered down to the way you died. To be immortalised by the one thing that proved you were mortal. Ooft. A Wikipedia page that I often come back to (what a grim start to a sentence) is simply entitled 'List of inventors killed by their own inventions'. It's a wild ride. A harrowing series of paragraphs that's just wall-to-wall occasions when someone's life's work just blew up in their faces. In most cases not metaphorically. There are the ways you'd expect, such as aviation, rocketry, medicine, etc. Basically, a whole bunch of European men in the 1700s lighting the wrong shit on fire. There are the famous ones that always pop up in conversation and we can never remember if it's a true story or not, like the guy who owned Segway and segued himself right off a cliff. (It's true, by the way.)

The entry that really breaks my heart is the one and only case listed under the subheading 'Publicity and Entertainment'. It tells the 1980s parable of Czech professional stuntman Karel Soucek. It seems that while living in Canada he had spent ages developing a shock-absorbent barrel into which he could climb and then be dropped from the roof of a stadium full of people into a tiny pool of water. One of his closest friends and rivals in the stunting world, Evel Knievel, publicly warned him against it, having called it 'the most dangerous stunt I've ever seen'. Which is a hell of a lot coming from the likes of Evel. But I'll admit, any advice was probably hard to take seriously from a man who spent most of his professional life either in an American flag jumpsuit or on fire. Nevertheless, Karel persevered. Plans were made, a show was put together and the night came. Thousands of thrillseekers and probably a few morons filled the seats of Houston's Astrodome. Soucek entered his contraption and was raised high up into the roof above the small tank of water positioned in the centre of the enormous stadium's floor. The whole thing sounds like some sort of Looney Tunes short. The atmosphere must have been electric. A countdown began but suddenly, through a tragic glitch in the system, the mechanism released Karel slightly too soon and as the barrel nosedived towards the ground it began to spin uncontrollably and hit the rim of the tank. Unfortunately, as it turns out, he had not developed a *completely* shock-absorbent barrel. Not at all. He had in fact developed a barrel.

This sounds very, very silly, but I genuinely think about Karel Soucek quite a lot. In some fucked-up way, the Soucek approach is maybe the best way to go. Here's a guy who believed in what he was doing, which was an insane thing to believe in by the way, to such a mind-blowing degree that he was willing to maybe lose his life for the sake of entertainment. That's a legacy. I mean, it's almost biblical. And imagine if it had worked. That would have been quite the journal entry.

Sometimes I look around our house and wonder if there is anything at all worth handing down. That's a bit of a problem with my generation. What are our heirlooms going to be? What are we passing along to be cared for in perpetuity? Am I going to be lying on my deathbed surrounded by my loved ones saying something like, 'This is the Samsung Galaxy I met your grandfather on. Look after it'? I do have one heirloom. It's a ring. My father gave it to me several years ago in what was an interaction completely out of character for both of us. It belonged to my great-grandfather, who also happened to be a comedian. It's been passed down to all the men in my family and I'm the closest thing we have to that right now so I'm just holding onto it tight until my sister transitions or something.

Of course, if all else fails and you're worried about not being remembered, you could consider the ultimate heirloom: a child. A living, breathing legacy who long after you're dead will be wandering around the place to remember you. Whether they like it or not. They could potentially even have your face. Now that's a two-pronged approach. Naturally, you can't always rely on them to paint a pretty picture. I remember years ago, my then-boyfriend-now-husband Kyran and I ventured deep into the Sydney western suburbs to be with my dad for a funeral of a much-loved elderly relative, his aunt. The few times that I met this lady she was the epitome of a firecracker. A hilarious Scottish woman who'd emigrated to Australia in the 1960s and when my father, an American, started visiting Australia in the '80s she and her husband had looked after him. These people had meant a lot to Dad and now they were both gone. We arrived at the church on what was a fucking steaming hot day and were greeted by my distant relatives. To give you an idea of the company, while holding small talk with one of Dad's cousins at the front doors of the church, I asked why she was using crutches. She went on to tell me she'd 'flipped her quad bike in the backyard after a few too many Green Monsters'. A Green Monster? I was told it was a Midori-based cocktail she'd invented. As we headed into the sweltering church, I thought about how soon her name would be popping up on that list of people who died by their own inventions.

The service began and we enjoyed the usual formalities of a church funeral. A lot of chat about how the dearly departed was 'home' and in a 'better place now'. Presumably somewhere with working aircon. Then it was time for the eulogy. The eldest son of the deceased stood up and made his way to the lectern. A tall, nondescript man who made couches out of the back sections of utes and once during a family Christmas had let off a smoke bomb he'd stolen during his time in the armed forces. What first struck me was that he didn't have any notes. Not even a couple of words on a napkin. As he started, it became clear why. He had not made a plan. Like, zero preparation. For about ten minutes this man um-ed and ah-ed his way through, completely raw-dogging it. At one point he said, 'Mum liked art . . . Right?' We were now all part of a workshop memorialising this man's mother.

Hours later at the wake being held around a pool, my dad called me over to join a conversation with him and one of my distant cousins. He was about nineteen, wearing chinos, an unironed business shirt, squared-off dress shoes and a lot of wax in his spiked blond hair. 'Show Rhys what you just showed me,' Dad requested with a tone I recognised. It's best described as bemused astonishment. He'd seen something bonkers and wanted a witness. My dad seems to have a knack for hunting out situations like this. He's always able to find something quietly unhinged going on in places you wouldn't expect. He's a divining rod for the suburban macabre. I knew I was about to see something wild.

I'm nonchalantly told this young relative of mine had recently ordered a home tattoo gun online. 'Oh yes,' I said, trying to act normal by pretending this was the fourth or fifth time I'd heard something like that this month. 'Have you done any yet?' I asked with widening eyes. There at a wake, as a pool noodle floated by, my second or third cousin put down his Malibu to unbutton his shirt and reveal a fresh and slightly crusty tattoo that went across his chest from collarbone to collarbone. In a poorly executed ye olde font, it simply read 'The Faster I Go The More She Likes It'. I stared at it and for a few seconds slipped into a sort of standing coma. It may be the most memorable image I have kept in my brain. No one's forgetting this guy.

Heading back home in the car with Dad, he mentioned how the tattooed youth had apparently recently broken up with a girl. *Good,* I thought. *She needs to move as far away from that tattoo as possible.* You can't be the person in a relationship with someone who has that permanently written on them. Something like that can really follow you around. No matter how hard you try, no matter how big your accomplishments are, you fuck one pig . . .

HOW TO WRITE YOUR FIRST BOOK: PART I

Hi there, buddy. Listen, this being my first book and all, I thought it could be fun, even a little useful, to drop by from time to time and let you in on how I'm finding it, as well as give you some advice if you're a first-time writer yourself. A sort of guided meditation through the process.

Oh wow! It's happened! You got a book deal. You clever thing. This must be a bit of a shock. Congratulations! I'm so proud of you. (If it helps, please feel free to read that last sentence back to yourself and imagine it's in the voice of some sort of paternal figure you've always been seeking the approval of in your life.)

You're going to want to tell everyone. So do it! What could go wrong? Once you've told everyone about this dream come true, now all you have to do is do it. I'm sure that'll be easy! Heaps of people have written books. You know, they reckon since the invention of the Gutenberg press in the 1400s, somewhere around about 130 million books have been published. That's so many books, you guys. While most of these are probably autobiographies of podcasters, reality stars and dangerous wellness gurus, some of them are actually quite good. Go have a look at a library. There are miles of books in there. Oodles and oodles of life's works stacked next to each other in a Dewey Decimal soup of knowledge, and if all goes to plan you are just a few simple steps away from having something you wrote sitting right up there with the rest of them. Your prose will be on a shelf metres away from an unhoused gentlemen who's making no attempt to hide the fact he is looking at some particularly noisy pornos on the free computers with one hand in his pocket.

I once read somewhere, probably on the calendar in my cosmetic dentist's waiting room, a quote by Robert Collier. He said: 'Success is the sum of small efforts, repeated day in and day out.' I don't really understand what it means and to be honest I'm not sure who Robert Collier is and I don't care to find out because he sure sounds like a bit of work to be around if that's the kind of shit he's spouting all the time. I suppose it's something to do with the idea that good shit comes from not expecting things to be handed to you, or that presuming you can make massive leaps forward without putting in a whole bunch of sustained work is delusional. So why not just say that? Yeesh, Robert Collier.

When trying to hit deadlines, I've been told it's super important to set up a strong labour schedule. So first, I'd suggest scheduling in a time to work one out. Drafting a secure timetable is good because it gives you the opportunity to go to a stationery store and drop a bunch of cash on a large calendar, coloured pens, Post-its and basically anything else you think you'll need in order to spend the entire day planning your plan. Take your time. Really relish it and start thinking about the standing desk you're going to use as you whack out some wicked prose. Make sure to tell yourself as you select each item in the store how useful it'll be.

When the first day of scheduled work arrives, get up to tell anyone you can how you're starting to get into it with the first draft today. Sit down at your computer and open a Word document. Actually maybe you could use some expensive app that authors use? Do a little research about that and buy one. Now you're ready. Title the file 'Book'. Nice and simple. Or should you think of a title now? It's important! Spend twenty minutes changing the name around and start to have serious thoughts about what the cover is going to look like. Oh, a Pinterest board will get the juices going! Nice. By now it should be about midday. Take a look at your file on the desktop of your screen. God, the desktop is a bit messy. You'll feel better and ready to work once you tidy that up a little bit. Actually, you know what would make this all easier? A keyboard that makes a kind of clicky-clacky noise. You've always been a tactile person and something that gives you that satisfying feeling in your fingers is going to make this whole thing happen a lot faster and make it more fun. Because if it's not fun, it's not worth doing.

To fill the rest of your afternoon, take quite a while to make a very complicated sandwich for lunch and then leisurely watch some TikToks about the symptoms of adult ADHD.

You're doing it. You're a writer.

CAMPING

I never had to come out. Not in any real way, at least. I guess it's because in order to come out, at some point one must be in. I've just always been like this. Some people have what could be described as a kind of luxury where they are able to wander the earth with no clear outward signs of their sexuality: people with shaved heads, anyone wearing dungarees, the entire region of Scandinavia. What lives they must lead, these sexy Rorschachs we can all project our horniness onto. Not me, though. For better or worse I am not a puzzle. I think for the most part people have always been able to take even a passing glance at me and get the gist. Then they hear me and that's all the confirmation they need. I've got this high-pitched lisp that won't quit.

I'm supremely lucky to have been born at the right time and more importantly into a family who just couldn't have given less of a shit. It was almost annoying, really. My itch for drama wasn't in the slightest bit scratched by the reactions I got from the loved ones around me. I'd employed some seemingly theatrical pauses as I came out to my sister, Ceara, as we stood opposite each other over the discounted

DVDs bin at our local Kmart. I waited for a reaction from her, but she didn't bat an eyelid and continued to trawl through the sprawling abyss of discs. Reflecting on it now, I can't help remembering the fact that since I was holding a double feature of *9 to 5* and *Steel Magnolias*, maybe that horse had bolted years before.

Telling my parents was slightly more complicated but just as uneventful. One afternoon when I was about sixteen I got home from school just in time to cut open a Zooper Dooper and settle in for an episode of *Passions* (vale *Passions*, vale), when my dad came up from his ceramics studio to mention that when leaving for work that morning, Mum had told him we all needed to 'talk about some searches she'd seen on the family computer, or something?'. He said it in that way many dads do: in a tone letting you know they mostly know what's going on, but haven't caught all the finer details. I stared back at my father trying to read his face for what was probably about three seconds but could also have been forty-five minutes. I genuinely don't know if he knew what was going on, but I did. I knew exactly what this was about because in the last few months we'd had broadband installed and I was doing my best to see each and every piece of internet porn there ever was. Reams and reams of it. Absolutely gallons of the most degenerate homosexual activity possible had been fast flowing through a phone cable directly to my optic nerve. Any time I could, really. It wasn't even what you'd call a hobby. It was more than that: it was a lifestyle. I truly thought I'd been covering my tracks by deleting the history as well as relying on the fact that neither of my parents were deeply computer literate. But it turns out there was something new called 'Autofill'. Mum had typed a letter into

Google and suddenly all the recent searches had cascaded down in front of her. This doesn't mean it was the names of the websites she'd seen. Oh no, that would be bad – but this was much, much worse. She had seen all the words I'd used to get me to this nasty business. When you're that age, looking at porn online is like cracking a safe, so she had seen all the disgusting little combinations and codes I'd used to get it open. All of this ran through my head as I maintained eye contact with my father. 'Oh yes?' I was able to muster, trying desperately to keep as cool as my rapidly melting Zooper Dooper.

'Did she say anything else?'

'Nope,' he shrugged. 'So we'll just wait until she gets home.' And with that he wandered back downstairs. I went and stood in my room dead eyed for the full two-and-a-half hours before Mum returned to the house. I paced and stressed. I'd thought about trying to relax, but my usual method is what got me into this mess, for Christ's sake. I heard the car come up the drive and she made her way into the house. It was quiet. Then there was a call for me to come into the lounge room. When I entered they were both sitting on the couch and I looked anywhere but them. For ten minutes we talked about the ethics of porn and how Mum uses that computer for work and how I shouldn't be embarrassed, blah blah blah. Not ONCE was the fact mentioned that the searches leant towards the masculine. It was just understood we all knew now and there were no problemos. Amazing. And infuriating. Where's the spectacle?!

I think my parents had always known. And were quite pleased about it, too, probably. They are artsy people. Why *wouldn't* you want a queer child? Imagine not wanting a queer child? Who wants straight kids? Ergh. Boring. To me it seems my parents have taken the stance of why have a pigeon when you can have a fun exotic parrot? I don't mean to offend any pigeons reading this but you have to accept you are the heterosexual of the avian world. I'm sorry, but it's true. I figure they just always knew. From a very young age there were some pretty definitive signs I wouldn't be for the ladies. For a start, I'm obsessed with women. Always have been. That's a red flag if ever I saw one. Loving women is just about the gayest thing you can do. Some of my happiest childhood memories are of sitting with my mother or grandmother while they ate meals with their female friends. Give me a table of house-white-wine-ladies of all ages and I'm set for hours. Of course, these kinds of interests in the fairer sex can cause some early confusion in the developing mind of a young boy. I mean, almost every queer person I know who grew up a boy had at some point in adolescence a poster on their bedroom wall of some scantily clad female pop star. Our fathers just the slightest bit proud their sensitive little guys had finally taken an interest in the female form. Oh, we had taken an interest alright. And we were spending hours at a time rehearsing the choreography in our bedroom so we too could look as good as Britney in a midriff.

The biggest warning sign in my case was that when I was little, I was just creepy. Just a creepy little guy. I know it's maybe the wrong thing to say, but I think we have to admit it: a lot of queer kids are creepy. It's how you know. All kids are camp, sure, but I was Disney villain levels of camp. A tiny, two-foot Jafar. At about seven years old I refused to call my mum anything other than 'Mother'. Yeah sure, she was patient at first but this, of course, naturally transitioned into the much more unsettling 'Mother dearest'. People would come over for dinner and not be sure if I was her son or just a little boy that died there in the late eighteen-hundreds. The line was eventually drawn when I tried to simply refer to her with her first name, Michelle. Mother Dearest Michelle reminded me she was my parent and not a colleague at the office. My love of the dramatic manifested itself soon after. As a preteen I was always sitting everyone down at family events to view what I called my 'plays'. A younger cousin might sometimes be presented as an opening act, but mostly I worked solo. The lights were dimmed and as soon as the show began it became pretty clear to the paying audience this was not a play at all but in actual fact just thirty to forty-five minutes of me accepting different awards. And I don't mean the well-known ones like Oscars, Grammys or even a Tony. I mean the likes of Critics' Choice Awards or The Kennedy Center honouring me for my lifetime contributions to the arts. I once got a Peabody. Some little boys my age wanted to be Spiderman, Batman or The Flash. I wanted to be Stockard Channing. A legitimately successful actress working mostly in theatre with a series of significant guest star roles in popular films and television shows. Let's just say that the signs were there.

I suppose the one person I ever had to come out to was myself. I realise that sounds like AI trying to write a Joni Mitchell lyric, but it's true. Just because everyone else seemed to be aware of my future orientation doesn't mean it was information available to me straight away. I think it's safe to say even in the most fortunate of situations, every queer person experiences at least the smallest bit of denial. It's a special kind of denial because it's a denial that you are in denial about.

Double Denial. The ol' DD. That type of fun homophobia that doesn't get shouted from car windows or drafted into policy. It lives right down deep in your belly. The internalised stuff – the strong stuff. I spent about a year around the age of fourteen doing myriad things to try and prove to myself and my peers that against all the odds and the evidence, I was in fact a straight boy who would grow up to marry and hold down a regular office job. Regrettably, because I was also so very, very, *very* horny, this manifested itself in some pretty weird ways. When standing with a group of guys at school I would regularly and unprompted bring up some straight porn websites I'd been looking at lately. 'You guys ever looked at creampiesexplosion.com?' They would stare and out of panic I would double down with 'Nah, it's great. I've used it to, ah, bat off to heaps. Been batting off a lot. You guys batting off much?' If you asked these people about me now they would probably say something like, 'Oh you mean that alien from a planet of perverts who was sent on a mission to learn the ways of human adolescent boys? Yeah, I hear they do comedy now.'

Even once I'd come to terms with it all I still went around telling people I was bisexual. Now don't think for one iota of a second this is in any way any kind of bi-erasure. You ain't going to see any of that over here. Bisexuality is of course a real thing and if you don't think it is you are so fucking boring. Not even offensive. It was offensive years ago. Now you're just boring. Weird and boring. But I just gotta tell you, I was not bisexual. My claims to be bi were the last couple of drops of the denial working their way out, so it still felt like good PR to have a foot in the other camp. This meant having a girlfriend. In retrospect I actually had a surprisingly high number of girlfriends in early- to mid-high school. But as I look back and have a think about it now, I'd imagine it was because they knew. Of course they did. They knew I was definitely not going to try anything. I was a safe bet. I'd go over to their house and spend most of the time chatting to their mothers about what a 'beautifully put together home' they lived in. So weird that their parents were fine with the bedroom door being closed . . . I do remember doing some kissing and dry humping. Remember dry humping? Such simpler times. Take me back there.

The dry streak, pardon the pun, continued until one fateful night at a party on my friend's farm, when my sweetheart at the time must have become frustrated and in a rush of hormones and Smirnoff Ices she preceded to grab my hand and just kind of jam it down her pants. It was a real shock. But I must say, not an entirely unpleasant one. I remember thinking *I can totally see the appeal here. I absolutely get why people like this.* But in the way you might see the appeal in doing a three-week sugar detox on a silent retreat. I can see why people do it; the results speak for themselves. But when it comes down to it, I just reckon it's not for me.

I truly do my best to not take for granted the insanely good run I've had when it comes to that side of my life. Inevitably I've had people call me a 'faggot' on the street. Not too long ago a woman shouted 'Poof!' from her car at me. I was shocked. Not because someone shouted, that still unfortunately comes with the territory. Mainly because you just never expect to hear the word 'poof' anymore. Such an old-timey slur. I kind of respected her commitment. It was almost nostalgic, like eating a Viennetta, listening to a *So Fresh* album or having any faith at all in the political system. I've been screamed at.

Shoved. Punched. None of it okay, but nothing compared to what has gone on in decades past to the older queers. They literally had to fight so we don't have to. Before I allowed myself to know any better, I used to feel like they resented us for that. It was as if the generations before us begrudged us for the leaps forward they made for us. And now I look at the new baby homos coming up. In a broad generalisation, it's hard for me to see them and not think about how free they are compared to my own experience. How unencumbered they seem to be by what someone might think about them. When I first started doing stand-up, if you were a queer comedian on a regular show you had to, and I mean *had* to, make a little joke at the top of you set about it. Gay men would usually say something along the lines of 'Sorry ladies' or some shit like that. It was as if, if you didn't allude to it, then the audience would spend the whole time you're on stage wondering if you knew. 'Why hasn't this person told us they're not quite right? I don't have a context for any of this!' These days I go to shows and see younger people hopping up and just starting. It's a teeny tiny niche thing but it's heartening nevertheless. Though the decrepit, bitter queer inside me occasionally finds it hard not to resent it. Don't these dumb little homos know what we did for them?

Never really having to come out about anything had always been a blessing until a couple of years ago when I accidentally came to terms with the fact that I am a non-binary person and didn't know how to tell anybody. To say accidentally sounds a bit reductive, but that's how it played out. I'd been conversationally wandering around the topic for years, but I always found a way to differentiate myself from someone who would actually openly say, 'I'm not a man.' Some queer people have a tendency to hold on to one identity, and don't always allow some of us to look much further internally once we've found something, which is understandable: 'I'm gay! That's fine! I've come to terms with that so we're all good now.' If I'd just crawled out of a well, why the fuck would I dust myself off only to carelessly lean over and peer down another on? A hidden little reserve of that denial can follow us around for years, and I'm still working it out. And I hope to keep on working it out. I've spoken to my parents about it, and as you'd expect, they're very on-brand and into it. No questions asked, really. I guess they figure, 'Why have a fun, exotic macaw when you can have a . . . whatever animals have confusing pronouns?' A meerkat seems right for some reason.

A BURDEN SHARED

Something I think about when I'm avoiding thinking about more important things I should be thinking about, is the hypothetical notion that if you were to drop me the way that I am now into my life somewhere between ten and fifteen years ago, I think I would most likely die. I was not living a particularly dangerous life. Not at all, really. I had just moved out of home and compared to some of my peers I was downright boring. There's just something about that age. At nineteen we have an in-built strength. It's a strange type of mental illness everyone goes through for the first two years of living out of the family unit. I'd describe it as a laziness of the temporal lobe, the bit of your brain in charge of making memories and emotions. As we have no real context for anything in the real world whatsoever, events and experiences just wash over us. We exist in a constant state of perpetually seeing or doing insane things that should be scarring us for life but instead we just think to ourselves *Well, this is fine* and keep swimming upstream.

By the end of autumn in 2009 I had been out of high school for almost twelve months, had been rejected by no less than three art schools, was living with my parents in Newcastle and I worked at a burger shop. It was pretty easy to see I was slipping effortlessly into a routine. Every day I would get up, watch TV for a few hours, go to work, be bad at my job, drink my pay cheque with the friends who hadn't moved away to uni, go to bed and repeat. Earlier that year I had been a finalist in Raw Comedy, a nationwide stand-up competition, and for the first time had been on TV. The next day I was back at the burger shop. I needed to get out of this rut.

I did some sniffing around and found out some schoolfriends who were living in Sydney were looking for a housemate to move in very soon. I made a snap decision to just do it. My parents were concerned but supportive – that's kind of their whole vibe. Once I'd finished a few more shifts at the burger shop, my dad helped me pack all my worldly belongings onto the back of a rented ute and drove me to my new beginning in the big smoke. With absolutely no job prospects or leads of any kind, I looked at the $2,000 in my bank account, an amount I knew was not enough, and thought to myself, *Well, this is fine.*

We arrived at the address I'd been given, and Dad lent a hand getting the boxes into the teeny tiny room. When we were done the two of us stood in the hallway, the air thick because there was no ventilation, as paint and chunks of wall crumbled because of rising damp. He hugged me, handed me $300 in cash, said 'Have a good time' and left. I waved as he drove away, shut the front door and wondered what in the fuck I was meant to do now. Standing in my bedroom, I looked over the four or five boxes and the yet-to-be assembled king single bed. Was this truly everything I owned? It had seemed like a lot more at home.

I wandered to my window and flung open the curtains with the type of gusto and drama you employ when no one's looking and you're pretending you're in a movie. Through the glass I could see into the backyard we shared with the four units in the complex of townhouses. There, standing like a ghost in the middle of the cracked cement was a shirtless man, who had to be in his late forties, using nunchucks. This was my first sighting of a man my housemates and I would go on to call Knuckles. He lived upstairs with his frightening dog. Knuckles stared into nothing with incredible focus as he swung and wove the nunchucks from one hand to another. The entire visible real estate of his torso and arms were littered with tattoos. Some were delicate and detailed while others looked as though they had been put there in a bit of a hurry by an alcoholic with a shake and a stigmatism. There was a lot going on, but one thing was without a shadow of a doubt: this guy was not good at using nunchucks. He wasn't helping himself, though, because around his neck hung a pair of old sneakers. They were tied together at the laces and slung around his shoulders. Why? Why were they there? He had shoes on. *Are they backup nunchucks?* I wondered to myself. *What's happening?* For over a decade I've been thinking about this scene, and the closest thing I can come to as an explanation is the phenomenon of seeing a pair of shoes dangling from some power lines that tell you that's where you can buy drugs. Well, maybe Knuckles, in a stroke of entrepreneurship, had decided to take out the middleman? None of this powerlines bullshit for him! Knuckles *was* the powerlines. Knuckles *was* the drugs. I closed my Ikea curtains, began to unpack and thought to myself, *Well, this is fine.*

I'd already decided this move signalled a change in me. I would be new in Sydney. First of all, I was going to be a smoker. All my friends had moved here and become smokers. On my first grocery shop I bought a packet of twenty-five Marlboro Golds. Having never really bought cigarettes properly before I went purely on the look of the packaging. The Marlboro carton looked like the kind hot people had in movies, plus someone once told me Golds had white tips instead of orange. Sold!

The first couple months of living in that house we were all on out best behaviour. We'd eat together, watch TV together. Laugh. So much laughing. This is how it always starts. Then the differences start to creep in. Suddenly everything isn't to share. There's a special quality to the food you eat when you first move out of home. In many ways it's predominantly a rebellion against what you grew up eating with your family. You take the food pyramid and just turn it on its head and start a food fight with your own metabolism. The first night I lived out of the family unit I went to the supermarket and bought a box of Coco Pops because I wasn't allowed to eat them as a kid, except on school holidays. I ate basically only Coco Pops until the box was empty three days later and I regret nothing/everything. Between the ages of eighteen and twenty-four I treated my body not unlike a Petri dish, adding all manner of different products and chemicals to see what would happen, and food was no different. There's no concept of textures or colour with that approach to eating. It's a hodgepodge parade of shapes of varying temperatures and salt content. Food is not for energy; it's to get rid of a hangover. There is an undeniable science to the food you leave in the fridge for yourself in the group living situation. It must be sufficiently okay-tasting to eat and cure a hangover, while at the same time not be appetising to the point a housemate might want to take it out and take a tiny piece off. This is a mistake people who work in hospo always make. They don't want to go near my beef mince that's so out of date it's almost alive again, but this dumb-dumb has just left a freshly made vegetarian moussaka on their allotted shelf and I don't want to victim blame, but they asked for it. I was the worst housemate on that front. I became a master at inching back the cling film of someone else's leftovers and through tactics I'd meticulously developed over years of being a freeloader, I went about spooning out small amounts of the undercarriage with a focus on retaining the structural integrity of the meal itself. I was making a carbs tunnel and essentially *Shawshank Redemption*-ing myself a full meal. Everyone's barking on about the melting polar ice caps but no one talks about the huge problem we face in our formative years of food erosion in a share house fridge.

After spending weeks handing out what felt like a thousand résumés, through some of the saddest nepotism possible I was able to land a trial at a restaurant through a work friend of my mum's. It was aboard a permanently moored sailboat in Sydney's Darling Harbour. The clientele were mostly wealthy and brash English tourists. A boat of English people in Sydney Harbour; it was like working on an immersive theatre experience about the dangers of colonialism. (Well, I guess working anywhere in Australia is that.)

During my first shift it quickly became clear that everyone else who worked there was German. They all chatted among themselves in their native tongue. I have nothing against the fine people of Germany, but we have to admit there is something very unsettling about a German whisper. It definitely feels like something is being planned.

Outside of my day job I was also starting to get stand-up gigs. Nothing flashy, but it was developing. As things flourished outside of the home, they were souring on the inside. Eight months in and tensions were palpable between me and the others, most of which was my fault. It could have been because of the food tunnelling but what's more I almost never paid for anything and was drinking so much after gigs that at least four times I had been found in the early hours of the morning fast asleep in the hallway with the front door to the house wide open. Fights started breaking out. Not loud ones, but quite intense words were said. In retrospect I was jealous of the lives my housemates led already. They both had good jobs and boyfriends. I was broke and the entire time I'd lived in that house I think I only brought someone home once. The king single bed wasn't exactly a natural aphrodisiac. After a show I'd met someone and, both a thousand sheets to the wind, I inveigled him into coming home with me. As was the etiquette in a share house, I'd put some music on. Without wanting to waste time I just hit shuffle on my computer's iTunes and got to the business at hand. A few songs later, as we were fumbling around each other, the track changed and suddenly I could hear a familiar voice. *What's that? It's kind of muffled. Oh, that's my own voice.* I thought I was having an aneurysm. What was happening? Suddenly I realised what it was. It was a recording I'd made on my phone a few nights earlier of me doing stand-up at a local open mic. Jesus Christ. In one swift movement I launched him off me. Without anywhere else to go because of the somewhat bijou dimensions of my bed, my new friend fell to the floor with a thud. Naked from the waist down I ran over to change the track. Pressing skip, I turned around to see my pal collecting himself on the floor and checking for carpet burns. It was clear the moment had passed. Standing there in the middle of the room Donald Ducking it as a drunk boy gathered his things and swiftly left gave me the feeling that things couldn't be much worse. Nevertheless, a couple of days later that exact boy texted to inform me he might have scabies and, as a precaution, I should probably undergo treatment. This involves covering your entire body with a medicated lotion – and I mean your entire body – that's left on for twenty-four hours to suffocate and poison potential skin-eating bugs. The time I needed to dedicate to this meant I lost my shifts at the floating restaurant. We hadn't even had sex. I did the treatment. Lying on my bed covered in goo with no money or job, I decided this wasn't fine.

There were two meals I ate frequently during this time of my life and here they are.

RHYS NICHOLSON

BREAKFAST

– SERVES: ONE. IT'S ONLY YOU –

– PREPARATION TIME: EIGHTEEN YEARS –

– COOKING TIME: TWO MINUTES –

– INGREDIENTS –

1 half packet Marlboro Gold Light cigarettes

as many scoops of your housemate's Moccona Classic Medium Blend freeze-dried coffee as you think you can get away with

boiling water

– METHOD –

- Once your housemates have all left for their workplaces, turn on the kettle and as you wait for it to boil, take this time to wander through their rooms and open some drawers. You're not looking for anything in particular, really – just looking. If they didn't want you to look they would have fixed locks to their doors.

- Once the water has boiled, make a terrible-tasting coffee and sit outside smoking three cigarettes in very quick succession. Have a small panic attack and spend the rest of the morning in the bathroom.

- Good morning!

A DEEPLY DEPRESSING BEEF BURGER THAT WILL MAKE YOU FEEL NOT VERY WELL AFTERWARDS

– SERVES: ONE. YOU ARE ALONE –

– PREPARATION TIME: TWO MINUTES –

– COOKING TIME: TEN MINUTES –

– INGREDIENTS –

500 g reduced-to-clear beef mince
some of your housemates' cooking oil (anything will do)
salt and pepper
½ red onion that's been sitting in the fridge for a couple days, peeled and sliced
some sort of cheese
Heinz tomato ketchup
Heinz American mustard
store-bought pickles

– METHOD –

- Split the mince into quarters and shape into balls. Put three of them back into the fridge because, let's be honest, you're eating alone. Get a glug of oil going over high heat in a non-stick saucepan that isn't non-stick anymore.

- Once the oil is shiny and smoking, place the hunk of mince into the pan and press down hard with a spatula until it's a flat patty about 1 cm thick. Leave it cooking for about 2 minutes. You'll know it's ready to flip when the raw side starts to bubble up some juices. It'll look like it's sweating. Flip it.

- Now that you've flipped it you'll remember you forgot to season it, so quick as you can add some salt and pepper to the now cooked side of the meat. Whack the onions into the pan and add the cheese to the top of the patty. Move the onions around a little bit. The aim isn't to cook them with any consistency, but more fry the taste of the fridge out of them.

- The room should be very smoky by now and it's time to accept you should have put the toast on ages ago. Toast always takes longer than you think it's going to. The meat is almost ready but this bread is a few days old so hey, give it a try. Turn off the stove, put a couple of slices of bread in the toaster and stare at it, fuming. You do this every time. Pop it up a few times to find it underdone, then on the last one make sure it's burnt. If you have the time, chuck that toast out and repeat this whole step exactly the same.

- Plate up by squirting entirely too much ketchup and mustard on each piece of toast. Stack the patty, onions and pickles on top, ensuring you fish the gherkins out of the jar with your fingers.

- Eat it standing up at the bench and then go lay in your king single bed to think about what you've done.

BREAKFAST FOR DINNER

When Kyran and I first started dating, I did literally none of the cooking. I have always been able to cook for myself, but at twenty-one years old the idea of cooking for anyone else gave me a bad case of the panics, so I just never did it. Like, never ever. I think he maybe thought I couldn't read, or something.

Carbonara was something Kyran would make us all the time when we had no money because the ingredients can be cheap and it can be made so quickly. For example, when he got home from working all day and I, having spent most of the day researching the voice cast of *Captain Planet* for no reason, hadn't made anything for dinner. It wasn't something we ever ate in my house growing up, and it blew my fucking mind. Looking at the raw ingredients of carbonara on the counter can make you feel poor, but eating them all mixed together and cooked makes you feel rich. It's the first recipe I felt like I could follow and not royally fuck up. Don't get me wrong,

I have absolutely royally fucked it up plenty of times, but that's the true, dreamy nature of carbonara: it is pretty bloody tough to ruin it to the point of inedibility. Even if the eggs scramble a little or the spaghetti is a tad beyond al dente, you're still eating fried pork, cheese and pasta. It'll still be delicious.

It's definitely one of those dishes about which many people, quite rightly, have very strong views. By no means am I claiming that the carbonara I make is traditional. It is, however, closer to what I'm sure Italians are serving each other up and down their beautiful country than what me and Kyran used to make. Look, I whack a little garlic in there and sometimes pop some flat leaf parsley over the top at the end. If there are some mushrooms in the bottom of the fridge that need eating, I'm going to fry them up and add them, too. Sue me. (Please don't sue me.) At least I'm not adding cream.

Don't mess about with the cheese. Use a nice bitey pecorino. It's in all the major supermarkets, so what's stopping you? And by 'all the major supermarkets' I mean one of the two major supermarkets we allow ourselves in Australia. Why not give yourself a little grown-up treat and get yourself a proper one from a deli? You've worked hard this week and you deserve it.

When it comes to your porks, I do my best to find a sizeable chunk of guanciale. It's the salty, fatty cheek bit of the pig. Think of it in terms of giving the piggy some buccal fat removal surgery. She looks fantastic now and actually prefers we eat it. If you cook it slowly enough the fat will render down and you won't need any oil and hoo boy it's making my arteries tingle thinking about it. But listen, pancetta will totally work, as will, at a push, some bacon. Just bear in mind that using bacon will make a nonna somewhere sad and she won't know why. Enjoy!

UNAUTHENTIC, BUT NOT OFFENSIVELY SO, SPAGHETTI CARBONARA

– SERVES: FOUR REGULAR PEOPLE OR TWO PEOPLE IF THEY'RE IN A LONG-TERM RELATIONSHIP –

– PREPARATION TIME: FIVE MINUTES –

– COOKING TIME: FIFTEEN–TWENTY MINUTES –

– INGREDIENTS –

350 g spaghetti
250 g guanciale
a couple cloves of garlic, peeled and crushed
4 eggs
1 heaped cup of grated pecorino romano, plus a little more for serving
freshly ground black pepper
handful parsley leaves, roughly chopped

– METHOD –

- Fill a big pot with water, then put a frankly absurd amount of table salt in there. I'm talking a handful. It should be enough that you're like, 'Jesus, this is a lot of salt. Is this right? It just seems like a lot of salt.' Get the water heating up and while it's on its way to boiling, book yourself a cardiologist appointment for next week and then get going with the actual carbonara.

- Cut your pork up into little cubes and whack those cubes into a large frying pan on a low-to-medium heat, stirring every now and then. I go low and slow with mine so the fat renders down all the way, but if you want, you can be impatient and go closer to medium heat. After about 5–6 mins, add the garlic, bump up the heat a little and keep stirring and cooking until the guanciale is to your liking. Personally I like it quite crispy. Remove from the heat and set aside.

- In a medium mixing bowl, pop in the eggs, cheese and a generous amount of freshly ground black pepper then whisk it up until you have a kind of slightly bumpy, creamy, golden sauce. Admire it for a few seconds then set aside.

- The water should surely be boiling by now. Cook your pasta. I'm not going to explain how to cook pasta. You're an adult. Check the packet instructions. When it's al dente, just before you drain it, fill a mug up with pasta water. Now drain your noodles and get them into the frying pan with the guanciale and garlic and turn the heat up to high. Get it sizzling and move the pasta around a bit so it's coated in the pork fat.

- Okay, we're here. This is the crucial bit. You can do it! (But also, like I said, if you fuck it up a little, who cares.)

- Here we go. TURN OFF THE HEAT! I'm sorry for shouting, but it really is so, so important that you turn off the heat. Otherwise you will have a kind of high-carb egg mess situation. Working quickly, pour the cream mixture over the pasta and just keep stirring, moving it around constantly so the eggs don't lump up. Stir and stir and stir. If after a couple of minutes it's still pretty liquid in there, you can add some more cheese. Vice versa if it's drying out: you can add a tablespoon or two of that pasta water. Doing this will also give it a nice shine, but be careful not to add too much. No one likes watery pork noodle soup.

- Serve it up and top with some more cheese, pepper and if you feel compelled, a little parsley. Eat it and good luck getting anything else done once you have. Have a nap. It's time for a nap.

MEET-CUTE

My grandmother once told me that she met my grandfather at a dance on a Tuesday, he told her he loved her on the Thursday and on the next Monday he'd asked her to marry him. When she recounted this I just couldn't stop thinking about how beautiful and old timey and just fucking nuts that is. Jesus Christ! Less than a *week*? Imagine that happening to you these days. Just try and imagine. If someone asked me to marry them after six days I think I'd find an excuse to leave the room very suddenly and then send a group text to everyone I've ever met and tell them about it because it's so royally insane to its core. But, hey, it worked out for Granny, and looking at some of the things I've done with people having only known them for a matter of minutes, who am I to judge?

Kyran and I have been together for twelve years and I tell you what, he puts up with a lot. It must be said the guy has staying power. I'm moody, at times hugely irrational, I'll do literally anything for a laugh and my refusal to acknowledge my lactose intolerance must make sleeping next to me a real cross to bear. Of course, there are parts of his personality that I have to deal with. He is incredibly stubborn, doesn't like Thai food very much, he's quite stubborn, he appears to be unable to get rid of a single piece of clothing and he sometimes can be very stubborn. But all things considered, he is definitely the load-bearing member of our relationship. If I do say so myself, we are one of those incredibly fortunate couples who seem to be able to just exist together. Without a doubt, like all relationships there are peaks and troughs and it's work, blah, blah, blah – but in the more than a decade we've been a thing we haven't really had any truly seismic problems, or a gentle swaying of the foundations of our relationship. That I know of, at least. To be fair, I often drift off while he's talking about boring things like tax, the news or his health, so who knows. Maybe we broke up years ago and I just haven't noticed. I am proud of the fact we have not once had an argument in public, we at least attempt to make each other laugh constantly and we're still in a place where one of us will go 'Woooooo' if we see the other naked. I've always thought we get on well enough that if we were characters in a premium drama, you'd probably find out later on that one of us was a rampant serial killer with the other completely unaware. Thank goodness in real life he works too much to have the time to install even a small underground locked room and I just don't have the focus to get my own credit card, let alone find out where to even buy cables ties, shovels and quicklime.

All this being said, it doesn't mean it was love at first sight. I'm not even sure I believe in that type of thing. It took us months to sort it out. We met at our mutual friend Zan's costume birthday party. He was twenty-three and I was twenty-one. This of course isn't really an age gap in the slightest, but you're changing and developing so quickly in your late teens and early twenties that two years can be responsible for huge differences sometimes. For example, as the years went by, he started getting hangovers well before me. Not too long ago he began getting a sore back and knees while I was still fine. As time trudges on it puts him in the position of being a living embodiment of a warning of what's to come for me: my very own 6'1" bespectacled canary down the coalmine. Speaking honestly, I have always found the idea of dating someone a wildly different age a little confronting. It's just not for me. Speaking only for myself, I think there shouldn't be enough of a gap that when one of you was a baby, the other one would have been old enough to hold you without adult supervision. I'm not judging you in the slightest, that's just my system.

The theme of the get-together we met at was Come As Your Favourite Album. Owing to my complete lack of musical knowledge I had decided to come as a greatest hits album. How did I dress up as a greatest hits album, you ask? I thought about it and thought about it and came to realise the best plan was to arrive looking like someone had beaten the absolute fuck out of me. Everyone was going to love it, I thought to myself. A massive amount of time was spent on this look. I'd used several tonnes of eye shadow to create a realistic looking black eye and accompanying bruises. Gory latex wounds were made and blended onto my face and torso. I ripped my clothes to ribbons and applied about a litre of fake blood to the huge amount of pasty white and surprisingly hairy skin that was now on show. I arrived, and then spent the next two hours explaining my costume to each and every person I spoke to. The idea was mostly met with wide-eyed fake laughs and then the topic was quickly changed. Devastating. The first person to genuinely laugh was Kyran, which made me automatically attracted to him. That was essentially my whole approach to romance at this time of my life. My internal monologue was a special mix of loneliness, lack of confidence and unwavering horniness that meant anything that could seem even remotely like interest at all from my potential future beloved's camp signified I was in. He could have been a 9/11 truther with an eyebrow piercing and a small tail, but a single giggle thrown in my direction and I'd be all, 'Thank you for this gift of attention. Do excuse me while I go full cylinders at getting you to be my life partner.' His nice head of hair helped, too. I decided to latch on and we stood at the party and spoke for hours. He was in no costume at all and looked great while my fake wounds were getting itchy. This was and continues to be a perfect metaphor for our relationship.

I all but missed the revolution of online dating. I had the Grindr app for about three months in 2010 and in that time it quickly started to feel like a randomised pen pal service with a series of racists who'd send you close-up unsolicited pictures of their penises that were so terrifying you'd expect the phone to ring afterwards and pick up to a voice saying 'Seven days'. The one time I ever got up the courage to organise a hook-up I was about twenty. As I left home I told my housemate at the time where I was going in case I was murdered and she knew to delete all my iMessages so no one ever found out what a two-faced piece of shit I really am. People worry about their sex toys and porn being found, but a good friend deletes the group chat you're in to talk about the other group chat you're in. She kindly obliged and we agreed she could have my Bluetooth speaker if something happened, but only after it was used at my funeral to play a muffled recording of me shouting, 'Help! Help! Let me out! There's been a mistake!'

When I arrived at the guy's house that happened to only be a short walk away, he opened the door and was immediately and very obviously disappointed with what had arrived. I came in and as we stood in the kitchen he offered me a drink. There was a choice between water and orange juice. He was drinking a beer: some of the most beautiful passive aggression I have ever seen in my life. I asked for an orange juice, he poured me one and then said he was just going to the bathroom. I suddenly lost my nerve and didn't really want to be there anymore, so I just left. And I took the orange juice. Hey, I had to get something for schlepping all the way over, and it was expensive juice. The nice kind you get from fancy grocery stores, with pulp. I think this is why I always struggled with dating apps. It could often feel quite transactional. What a thrill it had been to see the world through the eyes of a wish.com product, though.

Sometime in the afternoon the day after I met Kyran, as I gently cradled my hangover and tried for a third time to scrub the unyielding pink stains the fake blood had left all over my body, I got down to stalking him on Facebook. In my damp little room I sat in front of my laptop, opened Facebook and then realised I could not for the life of me remember his name. This is not uncommon for me. Once I'd found him, I added him and straight away sent his profile picture to my best friend at the time with the question, 'Is he hot or am I desperate?' Within minutes I received the reply: 'Both things can be true.'

The two of us become fast friends and as much as I thought I was laying it on thick, Kyran never seemed to notice. Finally and after months of me lamenting to our mutual friends that it just wasn't going to happen, while walking down the street our buddy Tom literally said out loud to Kyran, 'So, you and Rhys?' Something clicked and a further few weeks later after some dinner we found ourselves talking and drinking very bad wine in his bedroom. There's something very wrong with me in these situations – the moments when sex is absolutely on the cards. I will just kind of wander around the room and name things I see and tell stories that go nowhere. I think it's got something to do with trying to delay the object of my affection's finding out the vast difference between the idea of having sex with me versus the actual act of it. For coming up on twenty-five minutes, as he sat on his bed, I walked around his room picking things up, asking about them, pointing at something, asking about it. The final straw as I pointed at a plush Big Bird toy sitting on a shelf was 'You, you like The Muppets?' 'Yeah, I guess?' he answered with a tone that show how mystified he was about the fact I was still talking. I kept on going and heard the words 'Oh my god, have you seen the footage of Jim Henson's funeral? It's devastating' come out of my mouth. I wish I was making any of this up. Not even close to an exaggeration. Even worse, the next thing I did was take my phone, sit down on the edge of the bed and force Kyran to watch a four-minute clip of Big Bird with his hand resting on the coffin of his creator, openly weeping as he sang 'It's Not Easy Being Green'. No one would blame Kyran's dick if it went back up inside him to pack its bags and move to another city. Luckily, he patiently watched the whole thing, gently pushed my phone to the side and we had our first kiss. I had been anxiously making the whole scenario needlessly stressful and he had fixed it without making me feel like a moron. This was and continues to be a perfect metaphor for our relationship.

BEEF MELANCHOLY

Don't get me wrong, I love nice food. Food that involves a great amount of creativity. But let me say, having spent quite a bit of time with my grandmother growing up, some of my tastes veer closer to that of the Depression era. A special time for the tastebuds. Crunchy chunks of quick pickled onions in malt vinegar, tinned salmon with a little added malt vinegar, some deeply plain white bread with hard slabs of butter to sop up some malt vinegar. The fact some of our grandparents are still living after the sheer amount booze, cigarettes and butter they've consumed surely must have something to do with all the vinegar that seems to be in absolutely everything they were eating back in the day. They are the pickled generation.

Everyone has a strong reaction to corned silverside. Some people love it and some people really, really hate it with a vehement passion. There's no middle ground, it seems. And I get the hate, to be honest. I see the hate, I acknowledge the hate and I am holding space for the hate. This is undoubtedly a dish that you should never see as it's being cooked. A big lump of meat should never be seen so wet. It's unsettling and should be kept a mystery.

A dish, if you can call it that, like corned beef can hold a great deal of meaning for people. It's one that causes people to become very wistful. The first time I made it for Kyran years ago, in a shocking turn of events for me, and more so for him, he started welling up. Turns out his grandfather, whom he was super close with, had made it a lot when he was a kid. Now I make it for him often and there's absolutely some Freudian stuff going on there, but let's move on.

Most people like to have silverside with 'white sauce'. An accompaniment clearly named during a time when no one was willing to really admit or pluck up the courage to ask what it was actually comprised of. 'Listen, it's white so we called it white sauce and, frankly, I'm not comfortable with this line of questioning. Do you want to eat or not?' Along with this vague condiment you'll usually see some carrots and potatoes. A classic meat and two veg dinner is one of life's simplest joys, as is a corned beef sandwich. Especially when made by an elderly relative. The trick is: nothing fancy. A stone tablet-sized piece of tender silverside on white bread with butter so thick it looks like a slice of cheese. Add some pickled onions, firm slices of tomato and salt and pepper. Mmmm. Tastes like small goods rationing.

Oh also, if you happen to find yourself hungover and have some leftover beef in the fridge, it is perfect for frying up with some onions, potatoes, peas and parsley for a nice hash. Your hangover will thank you for the sodium injection and look, if it all goes south, it's the type of breakfast that comes up easy.

My mum makes a mean corned silverside. Recently I was chatting with her about the recipe and she reminded me that she uses mango skins in the broth. It brings a bit of tang and sweetness and, granted, it sounds absolutely insane, but listen to yourself – you're already boiling a piece of beef in a year that isn't 1952. Who are you to judge? Eat it up and bawl your little eyes out.

CORNED BEEF SILVERSIDE

– SERVES: ONE–SIX PEOPLE –

– PREPARATION TIME: TEN MINUTES –

– COOKING TIME: ABOUT TWO-AND-A-HALF HOURS –

– INGREDIENTS –

1.5 kg piece corned silverside
(I just get the ones from the supermarket, but if you wanna be schmancy and get it at a butcher, you go right ahead)

flesh and skin of 1 mango

1 large onion, peeled and cut into wedges

1 stick celery, leaves and all, coarsely chopped

1 carrot, peeled and coarsely chopped

1 bulb garlic cut in half lengthways

2 bay leaves

1 tsp black peppercorns

10 whole cloves

¼ cup malt vinegar

2 tbsp balsamic vinegar

a whole bunch of water

– METHOD –

- Take the beef out of the bag and give it a little bit of a wash under the tap to rinse off whatever the hell that is it's been sitting in. Brine, I guess? Its own blood? Whatever it is, it isn't right. Then place it in a big old pot with the mango, onions, celery, carrot, garlic, bay leaves, peppercorns, cloves and vinegar. So everything else, I suppose. Add enough water to fully submerge the beef by about 4 cm.

- Have a peek inside the pot. No, really have a look at it. Looks terrible, doesn't it? This is what everyone used to eat for decades. Wild. It's at this point I sometimes like to do a bit of stirring and pretend I'm some sort of witch trying to curse my enemies. Give it a go. Make your own fun, you know?

- Whack it all on the stove and get it up to a boil then straight away reduce the heat to low so it's simmering. Partially cover with the lid and keep simmering for about 2 hours or until the meat feels tender like a lover. If you were to jam an instant read thermometer in the meat it should hit 75°C.

- Once it's cooked you're going to want to scoop the meat out of what has now become a disgusting-looking pot of who knows what. Hold the beef above the pot for a few seconds to drain some of the liquid off and then get it to the cutting board for a little lie down. Slice it up against the grain and there you go. Delicious salty wet beef.

LEFTOVERS?

You're right, it's a lot of sad beef to eat in a day. A sandwich is the obvious choice, of course. Maybe you're cosplaying a postwar lady of the house so you make a nice big meaty boy with sauerkraut and pickle relish, all dripping in Russian dressing. Something your husband can take off to work while you're having a secret homosexual affair with a local barkeep. You know the type. Someone Kate Winslet could play with her eyes closed and maybe not get an Oscar, but definitely a Golden Globe.

Personally, I feel something with this amount of salt is wasted unless being repurposed to fix a hangover. So here you go:

MUMMY'S GOT A HEADACHE: BEEF MELANCHOLY MORNING HASH

– SERVES: FOURISH (HOW HUNGOVER ARE YOU?) –

– PREPARATION TIME: TEN MINUTES –

– COOKING TIME: TWENTYISH MINUTES –

– INGREDIENTS –

2 tbsp butter

2 large shallots, peeled and roughly chopped

2 cloves garlic, peeled and minced

2 cups potatoes, peeled and diced

¾ cup frozen peas

2 cups beef melancholy, diced

1 tsp dried thyme or rosemary (or both – go crazy)

salt and pepper

some chopped fresh parsley, to taste, for garnish

fried eggs to pop on top if that's your vibe (optional)

– METHOD –

- Think about what you've done. Now, in a large (preferably cast-iron) frying pan, melt the butter over a medium heat. Drop in the shallots and garlic then sauté (oh fancy) until the onion becomes translucent and the garlic is stinking up the place.

- Add the diced potatoes to the pan and cook for about 5 minutes, stirring occasionally, add the peas and keep it going for about another 5 minutes until the potatoes begin to brown and soften, like your brain.

- Add the diced melancholy and dried herbs to the pan, mixing well with the potatoes and onions. Continue cooking for another 5–7 minutes, or until the potatoes are cooked through and slightly crispy, and the corned beef has heated through.

- Season with salt and pepper to taste, keeping in mind the meat is already wildly salty. Please don't make a beefy ocean on a plate. Garnish with freshly chopped parsley in an attempt to make this look greener, fresher and healthier and not what it actually is: a pile of carbs and leftover meat you're about to put an egg on.

- If you want, pop an egg on there and eat cross-legged on the floor of your kitchen.

VERY VOCAL

When you work in the arts, criticism is always a given. We don't love it, of course. In fact we fucking hate it. But the clunky way in which creative work gets reviewed is unfortunately an unavoidable, and let's face it, integral part of the system. The way your work and abilities are scrutinised is not always from the likes of professional reviewers. It can come in all shapes and sizes. For example, on three separate occasions I have auditioned for and then not been given the role of characters in television shows who were written for, or in some way based on, me. I try not to let it hang over me too much but sometimes it does get to me that I am perhaps such a bad actor, I'm not able to rustle up enough of my theatrical aptitude to give a believable performance of myself. I can't help but wonder if maybe my family and friends wouldn't mind so much if a twenty-six-year-old acting school graduate with abs and good enunciation might step in and play me from time to time in real life. Even for just a couple days a week. Perhaps more if they were comfortable with nudity.

The job of an actor is undeniably a noble profession. There's no doubt about that. It's through the work of these artists that we're able to be taken to whole other worlds, to inhabit other times and ask big questions about ourselves as a species. Who are we? When were we wrong in history? How many hours of films can we dedicate to cars that are both fast *and* furious? (At the moment it's twenty-one hours and three minutes, but we all know they can't be stopped.) I've been lucky enough to have a few dramatic jobs in my comparatively short career. I like being on film sets. Everyone's taking it so seriously. All the cast members have always done heaps of research. Good actors do research and come up with backstories. If ever you've seen me acting in something, I want you to know that, no you haven't. What you saw was me, in someone else's clothes, standing in front of a camera as I waited for someone to stop talking so I could say my bit, then I'd be quiet while they did their next bit. At no point, even for a split second, did I believe I was someone – or somewhere – else. And to be honest, I'm at peace with that. I am friends with a lot of real actors and some (most) of them are outright terrifying. Think about whenever you see them in interviews talking about how they completely disappeared into the role. I once heard some award-winning guy say to a reporter about his latest Oscar bait something along the lines of, 'I don't even remember filming parts of it. I was so deep in there. I had to stay away from my family from fear of what the character would do.' Excuse me? I don't think that's as inspiring as you think it is, nor is it a metric of success we should be striving for. No one should be going around telling people in public that they are so good at their jobs they completely black out. Maybe it's time to have a little lie down and a chat to a professional because that's not cool. Artistic expression and storytelling are important and all, but we also need to admit that a huge part of the profession is simply mental illness with a publicist. I'm probably just jealous because the only thing my light neurodivergence has led to is elevated anxiety levels, and my partner won't let me near our taxes.

Any professional performer will tell you that voice-over work is the dream. There's no make-up, no costumes, you just read off a script and then they give you what can sometimes be a silly amount of money for the amount of effort involved. I'd always pined to be a cartoon character. When I was little I used to watch that opening scene of *Mrs Doubtfire*. The one where Robin Williams is in a recording booth flipping back and forth between different accents. I watched it and dreamt that one day maybe I too could voice an animation and if I worked hard enough, maybe I could even get a chance to recklessly gaslight Sally Field for custody of my three children. Unfortunately for me and my mortgage, on top of my limited acting chops, I can't really do voices, either. Anytime I take a whack at even the most innocuous accent, say Scottish or Dutch, it veers uncontrollably into something that sounds pretty unacceptable and at times could be misconstrued as being racially charged. So it's for the best that I just do me. If on the rare occasion I get a voice acting gig it's because exactly my voice is exactly what they need. This means you're never gonna hear me on a radio advertisement talking about how glad I am to have such-and-such insurance as now I have peace of mind my wife and kids are looked after if something were to happen to me. Honestly, the types I'm usually put up for are almost always some sort of cat or rodent who's either furious or stressed out about something.

Not all that long ago my dream came true and I was booked for a very exciting job. I was to be playing a character in the big national Christmas campaign for the department store Myer. Aardman, the studio behind *Wallace and Gromit* and *Chicken Run*, would be animating it. The rest of the cast was a slew of famous and somewhat recognisable voices from Australian comedy and drama playing sentient Christmas tree ornaments who, through a series of wacky situations, save Christmas. Frank Woodley was an elf, Denise Scott was an angel and Justine Clarke a mouse. Then there was me, a largely unknown comedian, playing a ditzy reindeer. Over the course of a few recording sessions we easily got it all in the can. It had felt fun, collaborative and not at all as ickily corporate as we were all expecting. We waited months while it was painstakingly hand animated and finally in November the ad was broadcast for the first time.

I loved it. It was cute but not overly sincere. They had put some of our improvised bits in. It was even being played before the new *Star Wars* movies at the cinema. It sounds so silly to be talking about being in a commercial like this, but I was just truly so thrilled to be a part of it. A few days after it had come out a friend sent me a link to an article she'd read in a small gay online magazine. There was a lot of long-winded yammering but basically the crux of the piece was that the voice on the new Myer TV spot was 'a stereotypical portrayal of a gay man'. They were saying this type of representation was lazy and problematic. I showed it to Kyran and we laughed a lot. Mostly at the very idea someone would have such a strong opinion about a Christmas ad with talking bits of plasticine.

Kyran is a good actor. Not on stage or in front of the camera but in situations where a slightly gruffer voice might be useful. I hear him talking to people sometimes and there's an ever-so-subtle difference in the cadence to his voice than usual – like how mums have a phone voice. He has a straight one. It's more authoritative. There's a huge increase in the usage of words like 'mate' and 'absolutely fucked'. It's not a problem at all. Nothing wrong with some low-key code switching to keep things moving. Once we had some renovations done on our house that had started while I was away on tour. When I returned, I witnessed the tradies, one by one, be perplexed by this person Kyran had visiting. He had in no way hidden me. He'd just said partner and they made the leap as they painted a dusty pink onto our kitchen walls. Maybe I was his camp cousin visiting from out of town. Then I would kiss him goodbye as he left for work and stand in the kitchen to offer our visitors a coffee as if to say, 'Any questions?'

As Christmas approached, another article/review of the advert came out, and then a couple more. All of them from pretty minor publications, essentially bloggers with enough money to buy an actual URL, but each and every one commenting that whomever this incendiary vocalist is who's playing this camp reindeer should think about what they're putting out there and, as one of them phrased it: 'This type of thing is throwing back the gay movement by decades.' Now look, I like attention and at times have been known to purposely cause shock for my own amusement. I've been accused of being too much by individuals before but that was from straight people and I usually just take that shit with a handful of salt because of course we can all agree straight people are en mass unhinged. It's always a true thrill to see part of the heterosexual community still be all spooked by the queers because we're doing our best to live genuinely, having been forced to wear our sexualities on our sleeves. It's still commonplace to be accused of forcing our lifestyles down people's throats when they're the ones who keep bringing up people's throats. Stop saying throats. You sound like a bunch of perverts. My favourite is the occasional time I still get called a faggot by some drunk twenty-year-old fuckboi who's wearing head-to-toe Zara. You can't call me that when you're dressed like that. Very pot calling the kettle a power bottom.

Noting else came out about the advert. No one proper took these critiques any further because it was a silly angle. I did, however, for my own mental and emotional wellbeing, ask my publicist to send a little something out to the individual bloggers/people owning laptops who had been so moved to write something. Just a quick note letting them all know that, in fact, that was just my voice. I wasn't even exaggerating it. It's just how I sound. And if they are going to pretend to help the community, pretend to be journalists, they should at least do their research, like any good actor does.

HOW TO WRITE YOUR FIRST BOOK: PART II

Okay, so it's been a few months and you're happy with a few of the parts you've been working on but if you're honest with yourself, maybe the words haven't quite been flowing like the River Jordan as you'd expected. Really more of a babbling brook at this point. You might be feeling a little angry. But hey, it's alright. Nothing to worry too much about yet. You still have ages, right? Yeah, absolutely. Keep at it, champ! As long as you're hitting those word counts every day, this'll be a breeze. You might even get it in early. Make sure you focus a lot on that. The word count. By focusing only on the quantity, you'll be sure to plant a nice toxic seed that this is what it's all about. Not the words themselves or the order they have been put in, but the sheer quantity of them. I mean, that makes sense. Why are people even buying books? It's because of all the words in them. Wait, *are* people buying books? Everyone always makes those jokes that print is dead, but it's not actually, is it? Lose an hour doing some research on that then convince yourself it counts as work and reward yourself with an afternoon browsing Facebook Marketplace.

By this point you will have been talking a lot about the writing for months on end and the people in your life will be interested in how it's going. When they show genuine interest in your progress – in one of your dreams coming true – snap at them. Let them know it's going fine but you don't want to talk about it. Allow this project to ever so delicately tap tap tap away at the bonds you have made with the people who love you most. If you've got a partner, I found it was a good idea to refuse to show them anything of what you're writing. You know it's just because you don't think it's good enough yet and want them to always see the best of you, but there's a pretty good chance this tactic will come across as confusing, mistrustful and potentially even a little hurtful. Lean into that.

You now find yourself at a crucial part of this whole endeavour. You had told yourself this day wouldn't come, but if we were to look deep inside your chest, we'd find that the truth is in there, that you knew reaching this stage was inevitable. It's time to let yourself wade into the warm, dark waters of dread and denial. Give yourself over to it absolutely. Don't let yourself think this is imposter syndrome. How could it be? Only someone who deserves to release a book could have imposter syndrome. You've made this bed, now shit in it. Become completely paralysed for days and probably weeks by the insurmountable enormity of the task you've set yourself. Permit yourself to entire eight-hour periods of literally doing nothing but staring at the same 800 or so words, moving them around as you stop to breathe and mentally manoeuvre away from a panic attack. The key here is to make a deal with yourself as you try to fall asleep tonight. Wager that tomorrow will be different. Peek into the dark abyss of your bedroom, taking long, bottomless drags of your weed vape (that is definitely not part of the problem) and tell yourself, *promise* to yourself, that this book of stupid comedy essays will not be the end of you and all the important interpersonal relationships in your life. Slowly drift off, the vape still warm in your hand, and have fever dreams about pulping mills and bookshop bargain bins.

Wake up far too early, or far too late, and repeat.

MR TAYLOR'S OPUS

A while ago I was having a drink and a chat with a close buddy of mine who is very, shall we say, sex positive. He's a good time gal. These types of friends are important for someone like me who's been in a monogamous relationship since I was twenty-one. He lets me know what's going on out there. He's my eyes, ears and penis on the street. We were yapping on about god knows what and for some reason I found myself saying something along the lines of, 'Well, we can all agree a man in underwear is far more attractive than a naked man.' To which he countered that this is absolutely not everyone's opinion and I 'probably just have an underwear fetish'. He said it so casually and moved on to something else straight away, but I was just left there sitting in my own brain and wondering if he was right. I wasn't completely closed to the idea. I've always been fascinated by the idea of people having fetishes. Closer to the morbid end of the fascination scale, probably. It could be argued that I've fetishised the idea. But it never occurred to me you could have one without knowing. And if that was a possibility, could it happen to me? I felt like I was someone on *Antiques Roadshow* finding out what they thought was their mother's jewellery box was actually where she kept her opium.

A few days passed and as I sat at a tram stop, I noticed an enormous billboard across the street. On it was a famous football player I'd never heard of wearing nothing but a pair of brightly coloured boxer briefs. He was lying back against a small patch of kitchen counter and barrelling the camera in that way people in these advertisements do. It's a plea to all straight women and gay men that if you buy this brand, there is a good chance this guy is going to come round to your house, absolutely rail you and then cook your breakfast on the now deeply unhygienic benchtop. I let myself stare at it. Inspect it. Scrutinise it. Was there anything about the underpants in particular that I liked? What even was involved in an underwear fetish? I guess I used to find the men's sock and underwear section of Kmart quite comforting when I was a kid, but I think that's because it was so close to the lolly aisle. I'd heard a story once from someone who was sleeping with a guy and, halfway through the grubby business at hand, the guy just grabbed his own pair of undies and smelled them. Like, really took a whiff. Good on him, but that's a level of narcissism I've never seen before or since.

Still looking at the billboard, I wondered if I was feeling anything. Anything at all? The garments themselves looked comfortable, I suppose. A nice fit. I don't remember how I know this, but apparently it's common on the set of an underwear photoshoot for the male models to have flattened-out slices of bread down their fronts. I guess it's to kind of round out the area. Create a bit more of a singular, organic shape and avoid any clear view of what exactly is going on down there. I have a lot of thoughts and questions. Of course the first place my mind goes is, well, yeast. But then moving quickly on from that, what kind of bread are they using? I mean we all love a nice chewy sourdough heavy on the gluten, but I can't help feeling in this scenario it just wouldn't be pliable enough. You want the slice to just ever so slightly obscure any obvious shapes. Not take over completely, just bring a level of uniformity to the whole area. If it were me, I'd be going with your basic run-of-the-mill store-brand white bread. It's square, white, durable and easy to work with. The Tom Hanks of bread. Just get a half loaf, though. These are underwear models, remember. No one's going to be wanting a sandwich later. Now what about the crusts? There's no question they are being sliced off unless you want some very confused customers bringing a whole new meaning to 'cut or uncut?'. But who's chopping them off? There goes my mind imagining some poor production assistant, straight out of design school and on their first day of a proper photoshoot. Sitting on public transport on the trip into work, this person lets their mind wander and they begin fantasising about what glamorous tasks their new career has in store. Only to arrive and find out most of the day will consist of cutting the crusts off some Wonder White to jam down the front of some angular-featured, twenty-three-year-old's Y-fronts. Actually, that doesn't sound too bad at all. Furthermore, I bet you could probably ask if you can keep the crusts you cut off. Pop them in a ziplock bag, take them home and you've got some lovely homemade breadcrumbs.

As this all ran through my head, I took it as a clear sign I did not have a sexually charged preoccupation for undergarments. And I was probably also a bit hungry. Truth be told, I was a little relieved I hadn't found my new kink. I'm not saying that in a shaming kind of way. Hey, whatever works for you. You do you. You do anyone. It's just personally, the idea of having to wrap my head around a whole new part of my sex life right now sounds like a lot of work. I just don't have the capacity to figure out new Pornhub search terms for myself at the moment. Plus, what if I keep going down some rabbit hole and suddenly I'm having to buy a whole bunch of contraptions to feed these new appetites? This all sounds like a shitload of admin. And when am I supposed to tell my fiancé? What's the etiquette here? Do I ease him into it after twelve years or have we been together long enough that I can just metaphorically grab the boxers and inhale?

For a long time, sex – of any kind – felt incredibly awkward to me. It was a very similar situation to when I first started cooking and having dinner parties. I'd always been able to do it for myself just fine. But as soon as anyone else was going to be there it all starts to feel a bit demanding. I mean, I like sex. Absolutely. Tell you what, gay sex is great. Rooting? Ooft, it's so good, you guys. Give it a try. Five stars. Highly recommend. Unfortunately, you need to be prepared, for it could take you anywhere between two and twelve years to get in any way good at it. When I first started even thinking about the idea of gay sex, it was a like a riddle. Sure, it's the same for everyone, but queer people come at a disadvantage. Pun intended. The problem is, no one told us anything. At all. Back in the day, there were a few rumours a couple of my fellow gay virgins at school had heard. What happens if you do this and what'll happen if he does that. It was all conjecture, though. No actual concrete conversation about how it all worked. If you had good enough internet you could try porn, I suppose, but even that wasn't much help. Is it too much to ask for these performers to occasionally mention something that would have been useful at the time? Some sort of advice that might equip us with confidence and know-how? A sort of training wheels for bodies? Something like 'Damn, this anal sex I'm having is so good because I'm hydrated, relaxed and focusing on my breathing' would have saved a lot of time.

Yes, of course, I know straight people were flying blind, too. Puberty is a blitz that spares no one. We were all just out there bursting at the seams with hormones and no one was talking about how we all felt gross and sweaty and stinky yet sexually enflamed to the hilt. And if we did allude to our situation, it was often not in a positive way. The most crisp, creative and hideous bullying I've ever witnessed was when a group of girls in my Year 8 art class asked one of their friendship group members, Sophia, if her teeth had started to come in. Rightfully puzzled, Soph asked what they meant and the collective went on to meticulously gaslight her into thinking girls eventually grow a cluster of small incisors in the inside of their swimsuit areas. For about three days they kept this going. I mean, sure, Sophia wasn't the sharpest tooth in the vagina, but it's proof there just wasn't enough unambiguous and non-judgemental information available for us to make educated, responsible and safe choices about our rapidly augmenting bodies.

I'm certain, and truly hopeful, things have got a bit better on the sex ed front in schools since. Frankly, they couldn't have been too much worse. I have a vivid memory of Mr Taylor, a PE teacher who was essentially a drawing of a PE teacher. A sun-damaged moon face in short shorts. I recall him standing there in front of us, a room full to the brim with puberty-ravaged fourteen-year-olds, letting us know that this very day would be the first in a series of lessons in sexual health. Bryce, one of the heavies in the back row who now works in real estate, piped up. 'Will it be a practical lesson, Sir?' A small eruption of laughter and hollers shot over the room as Mr Taylor rubbed his eyes and tried not to dwell on what could have been had his football career taken off. Speaking loudly over the top of us, Taylor ploughed through.

'Now look, do you think I want to do this? This is not exactly my idea of a fun hour, but it's important stuff and it could save your lives.'

Save our lives? Fucking hell. For the next few weeks this man stammered his way through the most fundamental, veering on Stone Age, basics of sex ed. Literally textbook stuff. He did this with very little interest or gusto and took almost no questions. This was a person waiting out the clock and intermittently warning us how something that we all understood to be very funny, was not funny and we should just grow up. There were a few times I got the feeling he went off book a smidge. Most memorably while reading a passage about all the different types of contraception, he suddenly went, 'Guys, I will say this once. Cling wrap and a rubber band does not equal a condom. And don't let anyone tell you otherwise.' He said it in a tone of almost contemplation. This was a man speaking from experience. This was a man speaking from the heart.

There's a specific sensation I remember experiencing when I went from being fifteen into sixteen. It felt as if I'd gone from having a virginity, to feeling more like I was lugging one around. There was a monkey on my back that was getting restless and I didn't like what he was up to back there. As the year went on there was a definite vibe at school of the haves and the have-nots as people's chastities began dropping like flies. The friends who were now sexually active in any way at all had a certain swagger to them. They all knew something we – the meek – didn't. A real Star Bellied Sneetches type of deal. It was now possible to be called a virgin as an insult. For me the experience was all very fraught because there was this thing I wanted to get rid of but I just had no idea in the slightest how to do it. Lightning struck when, closer to my seventeenth birthday, against all the odds, I found myself with my first actual boyfriend. He was tall, quite darkly brooding, had nice hair and went to another school. He definitely existed, contrary to what any of my schoolfriends said. We weren't together for long but it was with him, in a tent in the backyard of a party, where I made my first clumsy attempt to squash out our celibacy. While I'd not call it a complete failure, I would never say what happened was a smash hit. Without going into too many details, through some very impressive genetics on his side of things, the whole process felt rather like getting a round peg into a much, much, much smaller round hole. I remember thinking, if this is what this is, no thanks. It wasn't completely without its merits, I suppose. I was now officially in a sexual relationship. There was at least half a star on my Belly and I was allowed to have a little bit of swagger. Unfortunately, a few weeks later my betrothed had conversationally mentioned, out of nowhere, that if pushed to it he reckoned he could take someone's life. So we parted ways.

Over months and years, right into my twenties, I continued to always find intimacy pretty awkward. Every time I did it, which for stretches of time was quite often, I would nervously say dumb jokey things, be anxious and all-round peculiar. I refused to take off my shirt for the first three months of Kyran's and my courtship. I was essentially always in a state of apologising for what I was doing and the fact that I was even there doing it. It had turned out Mr Taylor had in fact imparted practical lessons – far too practical. There was such a bias towards practicality that it was impractical. The entire focus was on the 'what' of sex with zero priority on the 'how' or 'why'. This is kind of how I feel about school as a whole, really. High school is a long walk for what we actually leave there with. What life do they think they are getting us ready for? There should be a class that's just called Life Stuff. You go in three times a week and for an hour they take you through a bunch of shit no one ever mentions that would have saved a lot of time had you known. If you really wanted to prepare me for the world, how about a little less chat about Pythagoras and maybe mention once or twice how in the fuck tax works. Do I really need to know about photosynthesis, or would it be better if you'd told me to never stay at a party attended by more than two white people with cornrows. Maybe it's not sexual education but more a case of 'Being a Person, Education?

After a lot of thought, plus a few rather intrepid wanderings around some of the more sexually unprejudiced arenas of the internet, I have come to realise (by *not* coming, as it were), I do not have an underwear fetish. Writing this has helped me arrive at the notion that if I do have a fetish, something that really gets me going, it's the very idea of clear and non-judgemental sex education. It should be about the importance of honesty and behaving respectfully, even to the extent that there's a passing mention about the seriousness of full consent. And most critically, no matter who you think you are and what sexuality or gender you find yourself in, do not at any point attempt to have penetrative sex in water. It just doesn't work. Everyone needs to stop pretending it does. Definitely stop putting that shit in movies and TV shows. Will we ever know why as soon as semen hits water it becomes cement? Who can say. If you take anything from this entire book, it's don't have sex in water.

CONFUSED UNDERWEAR MODEL CHICKEN SCHNITZY

It's safe to say the seemingly endless lockdowns we suffered through during the small global health crisis that kicked off somewhere in the last decade (I no remember exactly when it happened after my brain no work so well because of we in house too long time) served up a firm wallop of existential dread. Mainly because of all the, you know, death. But as time trudged on and as days turned into weeks, weeks turned into months, months turned into kilos and kilos turned into eating a bucket of fried chicken in the bath, I think what truly started to get to us was how we had lost the unassuming flickers of satisfaction in our daily lives. Nothing bonkers, mind you, just the mundane pleasures of, say, popping to a grocery store whenever you fancy it, or knowing what the lower half of a stranger's face looks like, instead of pleasure morphing into having to wait until your partner goes on their restricted-to-one-hour-walk so you can frantically knock one out in the shower then have a little cry. Just the quiet little events in your regular week, during the before times, that seemed so simple you had no idea you were taking them for granted.

One of the lifestyle absentees that we truly, deeply missed in our home was the simple pleasure of a pub dinner. There's something about it.

My go-to bistro meal is the humble schnitzy. Preferably the size of my head and prepared by a kind yet furious older woman wearing a polo shirt with the pub's logo on it who has a husband that promised her a different life.

I made a lot of schnitzies during the covid hibernation period purely to feel some degree of sense memory. Sometimes it was as if Kyran and I were doing some complicated, non-sexual roleplay where we weren't at home at all, but actually in a busy outer-suburbs pub dining room. We'd compile a playlist of bad acoustic covers and I would make the enormous crumbed chicken breasts with accompanying chips and over-dressed green salad, then emerge from the kitchen in an apron. As Kyran looked up I'd slam the plates, laden with far too much food, onto the table and announce, 'The cutlery, sauces, salt and pepper are over there on the counter and water is self-service.' He would nod politely and just before I headed back to the kitchen to get out of character I'd continue, 'There's also half-price pints tonight and a band on later.' We may never know the true extent of the injury our brains acquired over that period. Frankly, I don't care to know.

– SERVES: FOUR –

– PREPARATION TIME: ABOUT THIRTY MINUTES –

– COOKING TIME: TWENTY–TWENTY-FIVE MINUTES –

– INGREDIENTS –

2 large eggs

1 clove garlic, crushed

1½ tbsp decent Dijon mustard

4 skinless chicken breasts

2½ cups panko breadcrumbs

¼ cup finely grated parmesan

zest 1 lemon

about 1 cup plain flour (you might need more)

vegetable oil

1 lemon cut into 4 wedges

handful of fresh continental parsley, chopped

– METHOD –

- In a medium bowl whisk together the eggs, garlic and Dijon. Set aside.
- To flatten out the breasts (lol), put the chicken breasts in a ziplock bag or between a couple pieces of plastic wrap and whack them

gently with a meat mallet (lol) or rolling pin until they're an even thickness and vaguely uniform in girth (lol).

- To make your crumb, combine the breadcrumbs, parmesan and zest, then spread onto a plate.

- Sift the flour onto its own plate.

- Now line up the plates with the egg mixture in the middle to create a little production line. One breast at a time, coat each piece in flour on both sides and shake to get rid of any excess, then dip into the eggy mixture, coating it thoroughly, and hold it above the bowl for a few seconds so any excess drips off. Now lay on the plate of crumbs, gently pressing down on each side to get every nook and cranny breaded. Transfer to a tray and pop in the fridge for 20–30 minutes. Be sure to remove it about 20 minutes before cooking so the chicken can return to room temperature. No thank you, raw chicken in the middle. No thank you.

- In a big ol' frying pan large enough for two pieces of chicken, heat 2 cm of oil until it's shimmering on top. Working in batches, fry the chicken for about 5 minutes on each side. Your schnitzies should be crispy and golden, but not too dark.

- Serve with lemon wedges and parsley sprinkled on top.

BIG DEAD ENERGY

I don't really believe in many things I can't see: God, spirits, a decent Jennifer Aniston vehicle. None of it has ever seemed legit. Not because I think I'm above it all – I just can't be bothered. Who has the time these days to have faith in anything? I barely believe in myself, and I can see me. However, a few years ago while touring in Tasmania I found myself on a local ghost tour. Why? Because I work in an industry that demands constant creative output and it's getting to the point that I am flat-out running out of shit to say. We all know the internet has ruined everything, but to me there is no clearer evidence of this than the sheer amount of material having to be created to sate us, the doomscroll generation. I used to want to be a writer. A proper classy writer. It sounded incredible. It seemed like all you needed was a pair of thick-rimmed glasses, a bottle of brown liquor and an emotionally unavailable bisexual lover, then you'd be set. Biopics and premium dramas about the likes of Truman Capote or

Gore Vidal had promised me a life of glamorous parties, cigarettes and hurtful comments shot between my cerebral friends. The work of a wordsmith appeared magical because it seemed to involve very little actual work. Then the world wide web came along and fucked it all up for everyone. No longer could we dream of banging out a classic and full-on Harper Lee-ing it before hitting the coast to catch up with our pals at the summer house for cocktails in light linen leisurewear.

These days, if you want to write professionally and profitably, you'd better have half a dozen articles ready with a headline along the lines of 'We've Been Eating Oranges All Wrong' or 'How the Novel Coronavirus Changed The Way I Talk To My Birds' or '10 Reasons You're A Dumb Little Bitch, You Dumb Little Bitch'. It must be exhausting to find yourself in the position of having to produce an ever-flowing river of opinions like this. I mean, I'm only human; there's a finite number of angles I can have on the cultural ramifications of NFTs. If I'm honest, I am still not completely clear on what an NFT actually is but I keep hearing the term being thrown around so I thought I'd mention it here to seem hip. Thus proving straight away I am not.

On some level I can relate to the content creators of the world as I've had not dissimilar troubles myself when trying to put together new stand-up material. Every year when I sit down and put fingies to laptop and write a new show to tour, I'm smacked over the head by how few beliefs I actually hold. Once you've exhausted your impression of your mother and told an audience how you lost your virginity, a stand-up can quickly begin a steep downward spiral to the bottom of the barrel unless you keep trying to make interesting things happen in your life. I often spend a not inconsiderable amount of my time doing a bunch of stuff that doesn't feel very good purely for the sake of five minutes of dumb comedy. It's my system and it's this system that led me to joining a group of paranormal fanciers as we went on a guided walk through what was sold as a place wildly overcrowded with throngs of spirits with unfinished business, but in reality was essentially a sewer.

In a small, semi-regional town I found myself having been away from home for coming up on three weeks and was beginning to go a little loopy. I'd been hopping around doing gigs and staying in some of the less salubrious motels this wide brown land has to offer. I must admit, I like a nice hotel, but I truly love a shitty motel. Shittier the better, if you ask me. Places where 'television' and 'fresh linen' are listed on the street sign as if they're fancy amenities. Situations where you wouldn't be surprised if the number for Lifeline is embroidered on the towels. There's something very freeing about knowing that whatever you're up to in your $49/night glorified cell, it doesn't touch the sides of the worst thing to have ever happened within those four walls. Not even close.

Being paid to tour the world telling jokes is literally a dream come true, but it can be a lonely life. I know the depths of loneliness have been reached when a sense of paralysis sets in. I'd spent the previous night lying in bed as a couple next door engaged in loud, terrifying sex, the sort you only have in a hotel. (What is it about hotels that bring on that level of passion? What is it about renting someone else's bed that makes us turn into ravenous root rats? Is it an expectation thing; do we feel like we have to? It's as if as soon as the person at the front counter says 'Enjoy your stay', the countdown to unhinged hotel intercourse begins. You'll do things that would never occur to you to do at home. You're going to commit some horrible acts in there. You're going to disrespect that room. If hotel rooms could talk, they wouldn't. They would be weird and quiet because they've seen too much in their lives. Like the little Amish boy in *Witness*.)

Lying there between the over-starched sheets as a cacophony of moans and expletives leaked through the thin walls, I made a deal with myself that the following day I wouldn't just sit in my accommodation trying to view the whole internet. I didn't have a show so I would go out and do something. See something. Have an opinion about the world. A quick google about the area revealed that pickings were slim. If I was compelled to leave my room, I had the choice of an agricultural museum, something called Trampoline World and the ghost tour. Having never once wondered a single thing about tractors and then considering the optics of me, a lone twenty-five-year-old, turning up to a world of trampolines, I booked a spot online for the afternoon session of the spooky, spooky tour. Information about what was in store was a bit scarce, but I remember hoping the guide was contractually obliged to wear a costume – even just a spattering of fake facial hair. I love it when they wear a costume. It's the same reason I love themed restaurants. I like to see acting students in their natural habitats.

The majority of our jaunt into the unknown would take place in the underground tunnels/storage areas of an old hotel that was said to be one of the most haunted places in the country and perhaps the world. Looking back, this is basically just a fun way of saying 'one of the most visited places in the world by people who have "Magic Happens" bumper stickers on their cars that they sometimes live in'. I counted three of them in the car park when I arrived. The hotel itself was grand and old, but in that quintessentially Australian way – think less Vincent Price and more local repertory production of *The Man from Snowy River*. I reckon I've seen spookier real estate on the Sydney rental market. When I got inside I joined a group of about eight that had begun gathering around a marked assembly area in the lobby. The bunch was who you'd expect to be there: a few couples in their sixties and seventies long since sick of each other and there purely to do something, anything at all, so they have a topic of conversation tonight as they eat and complain about a bistro meal; a couple of European tourists who I think were staying in the hotel and didn't seem to be all that clear on what they were there for; and finally, of course, no guided tour is complete without some white guy in his mid-fifties who probably couldn't convince his family to attend with him so has come alone on principle. Someone I would describe as a real Brian. The woman behind the hotel reception desk told us our guide would be along soon, so we stood around for a few minutes and waited. The boomer loner tried around four or five times to get a conversation going with everyone to absolutely no result. Just standing there shooting his shots over and over again with random statements about the place and the day. He was getting nothing apart from a few polite smiles from the Europeans.

Finally we were greeted by our escort into the eerie unknown. In an effected accent he introduced himself as Simon. I'm not sure what I was hoping he'd be called, but Simon was not it. Maybe Thomasin?

Or Heathcliff? Or something more abstract like Mop? The name Simon doesn't exactly conjure the dark arts or a general feeling of the heebie-jeebies. It summons poly-weave business shirts and thoughts of tax time. Simon was about thirty-five, had eyeliner on and wore a three-piece op-shop suit with a pair of converse shoes. This wasn't the type of costume I'd been hoping for. He looked like Dr Whos' slightly intense cousin who lives in the country. Dr Whom. There was a little bit of an introduction explaining that the place opened in the 1920s, was once a grand, stately home and then we were off outside and through a door at the side of the building and down a flight of stairs into the undercarriage of the hotel. Lined up in a stony basement like the Romanovs, Simon asked us if we felt anything different between in there and outside. Well, *yes, Simon*, I thought to myself. *We're* in*side now. It's heaps different.* Some lady replied that there was a bit of a different vibe now we were surrounded by concrete. 'That's because there are spirits in here,' declared Simon as he waltzed into the next room with panache. Around this time I realised there probably isn't any formal qualification for Simon's line of work. I mean, to be a guide at, let's say, an art gallery or a history museum, I'd imagine it helps to have some knowledge about art or history. Had I gone to the agricultural place I'd have hoped the host might have at least seen a piece of farm equipment before. As it turns out, to usher a crowd through a potentially haunted site, your only preparation seems to be thick eyeliner and a weird verbal cadence.

As we travelled from room to room, Simon continued recounting tales about the ghouls that were said to be living in the walls. One of them was called Ol' Jim (not even joking). Ol' Jim was an apparition that had been spotted numerous times by hotel staff. He apparently wore a plaid shirt, hiking boots, and had been known to push men around. When I asked who Ol' Jim was, Simon remarked, 'We actually have no historical documents to confirm who Jim might be.' This sent the group into a tizzy of visible unease while I was left wondering what was so fucking scary about a possible clerical error.

Over the next fifteen I became more and more frustrated by the way this was going and I think it showed. I can't be sure, but I have a feeling Simon and the rest of the group didn't like me very much. I'm only basing that on their reaction and collective demeanour towards me. It could be because they sensed I was a skeptic but it's more likely owing to how I gave myself the job to be disruptive throughout the entire tour. I can't tell if it was the loopiness I was feeling from being away from home or if I'd just snapped and felt like this guy was wasting my time and money. I asked questions like, 'How do the spirits feel about the review bombing and general treatment of the all-female reboot of *Ghostbusters*?' and whenever possible I would say loudly 'Ghost tour? Oh no, there hasn't been a ghost tour round these parts in over forty years.' Then I would laugh maniacally. This was received with near silence every time. Even the Europeans stopped smiling. Around the latter half of the 90-minute paid-for hostage situation my mind wandered right off. I decided that if I were a ghost, a hotel would be the best place to haunt. You'd never be bored! There's a constant flow of different people coming and going. Conducting their odd little business, thinking there're alone. Nope. I'm in there. Just having a little lookie loo. Then I got to thinking, in all this chat about hauntings, where in the fuck are all the ghosts of people who died within the last twenty years? The ghost stories you tend to hear all begin along the lines of ''Twas the year 1809. She was a milkmaid and a ship fell on her sailor husband so she threw herself down a well and now they haunt this harbour warning strangers of the perils of love.' It's never, 'In 1997 she ate some chicken that wasn't quite cooked and she shit herself till she died. They say you can still hear her voice around the deli section warning you to check the date . . . check the date . . . the date . . . date.'

The rest of our journey turned into more of a real estate tour. It was less 'the dead live' and more 'take note of the fine fittings and trim around the windows'. There was a feeling by the end that maybe we were meant to make an offer on the property. As we were saying our goodbyes I suggested that when we die we all meet up here to catch up for old time's sake. No one laughed, although the Brian genuinely seemed to be into the idea.

After all was said and done it was near enough to dinnertime so on my way back to my motel I went to the local Chinese takeaway every small town in Australia has. You know, the one run by a Greek family. My plan was to get back to my room, get a bit drunk and continue my surveying of the internet. With my practically glowing sweet and sour pork in hand I wandered homeward and as I passed the reception, who do I see but Brian. I couldn't hear what was going on exactly, but he was leaning on the counter and chat, chat, chattin' away to the pretty twenty-something girl on duty. He wasn't being creepy or anything. As he spoke and laughed at his own attempts at humour, just like earlier underneath the hotel, he got almost no reaction from his audience. She was nodding and occasionally smiling but really just looking through him. This pale, invisible figure trying desperately to make contact with the other side. This was the real haunting. I had seen a ghost that day after all.

MEDICINE

I remember being very excited by the idea that I would be drinking booze for the first time. A couple of friends and I thought about this momentous occasion and instead of going the usual route of some Smirnoff Ices or Vodka Cruisers or goon, we decided to be creative and instead make vodka spiders. Yes, you read that right. We asked our friend with a fake ID to buy us a big ol' bottle of *very* affordable vodka, we bought ourselves a selection of flavoured soft drinks and a large tub of plain vanilla ice cream. At a party with a bunch of older kids we then proceeded to make our chosen libations as if they were classic cocktails. We called them 'Specimens' because they were spiders that had been spiked. Around three hours later, one by one we joined each other in the back garden to absolutely hurl our insides out. To this day the sight of a family-sized ice-cream tub makes me light-headed.

There is something very nice as an adult about having a drink order. Something you can ask for with confidence at a nice bar and be able to manage any follow-up questions from the bartender. Will we ever understand why bartenders in nice bars want us to be as confused as possible? I've been confidently drinking for the better part of twenty years and sometimes the person working behind a bar will have so many vaguely condescending follow-ups I get so confused it starts to feel as though I've been shaken awake from a coma and asked what type of gin I'd like.

Over the course of the last decade or so, as I have annexed the job of the cooking in our home, Kyran has taken to the role of bartender. A responsibility arguably as, if not more, important when you're entertaining. In no way am I saying this is a new thought, but at the beginning of a night as guests arrive, the drink offered on entry is pivotal. It's the courtesy finger that potentially sets the tone for the entire evening. During that small global health crisis we had, Kyran and I found ourselves indoors quite a bit doing our best to gain around 10 kg, mostly on our faces. Having recently opened a bar in Melbourne's CBD, we were in the unenviable position of beginning the pandemic as the arts and hospitality businesses absolutely collapsed, so we had nothing else to do but weep self-pitying tears and drink a commercially stocked bar amount of booze. At all times we had eight coupes chilling in the freezer for 4 pm when it became not so much 'cocktail hour' but closer to 'cocktail what amount of time it is until I fall asleep somewhere in the house'.

Negronis, as our lord and saviour Stanley Tucci taught us during this difficult time, are always a righteous choice. They are classy and impress dumb-dumbs because they taste harder to make than they actually are. Personally, I'm always going to lean on a martini. To me, a teeny tiny martini (a mar-tiny) is the greatest start to the night because it feels grown up and can really bring a particular energy to the conversation. Makes everyone into a real Chatty Cathy, does a martini. It's like an EpiPen. Only one though; no one should be having two martinis before dinner, no matter how teeny tiny these martinis. And I'm talking regular martinis, or small variations of the classic. No espresso martinis, please. If you want your guests to talk loudly and have diarrhoea in your house, just bite the bullet and give everyone some blow. At least then someone might offer you a stake in a business they've just manically decided to start.

At a bar or a nice restaurant I usually order a classic dry gin martini with a twist, but for some unknown reason at home I always prefer a Perfect Martini aka a Medium Martini. It's delicious and a little less intense than a dryer boy, which means it's a nice gateway drink to bigger kid versions.

The other tipple we let swallow us whole during the covid times was a manhattan. I don't know why we aren't all drinking manhattans all the time. Everyone's been all full steam ahead on old fashioneds in the last few years and the manhattan just feels a bit more boozy and fun. It's like the old fashioned's divorced aunty. I should warn you, though, they will get you fucked up. For something named after a place that apparently never sleeps, she's a good nigh nighs goodbye possibly forever drink. Sometimes the maraschino cherries can be hard to find, and if that's the case then you can absolutely make them yourself if you're feeling crafty and showy. I mean sure, why not? It's not *that* hard, but you have to pit the cherries and they take a while to be ready, so whenever I see them in a store I buy a jar and keep heaps of them in the pantry for when friends (me alone) want to have some cocktails (drink by myself).

A PERFECT MARTINI

– INGREDIENTS –

1½ shots nice quality dry gin
½ shot dry vermouth
½ shot sweet rosso vermouth
1 lemon

– METHOD –

- Fill a tall mixing glass with ice and add all the wet ingredients. Stir until absolutely fucking freezing and strain into a pre-chilled coup. For garnish, I like a button of lemon that you can express over the top before dropping into the drink.

MANHATTAN

– INGREDIENTS –

2 shots good quality bourbon
1 shot sweet rosso vermouth
dash angostura bitters
maraschino cherry

– METHOD –

- Fill a tall mixing glass with ice and add everything but the cherry.

Just as with the martini, stir it for a few seconds until it's as freezing as a far-off icy stare from Nicole Kidman in *Cold Mountain*.

- Dip the stirring spoon into the jar of cherries so there's a layer of syrup on it, then give the cocktail another quick stir.
- Strain into a chilled coupe and plop a cherry in there. Drink three in quick succession and fall asleep standing up.

ALL HAIL THE POLITICAL CORRECTNESS BRIGADE

Over the last few years there has been a train of thought gaining traction around the place that never ceases to thrill me. It's something that has always been present in some way or another, but it's really been getting some airtime of late. I'm talking about the idea that there is a guided and structured conspiracy to obliterate straight white men. Particularly in the entertainment industry. 'We can't say anything anymore! We're being silenced!' they scream to packed theatres and from inside their multi-million-dollar media deals. 'It's political correctness gone mad! We've had the rug pulled out from under us!' they yelp as someone frantically weaves another rug to put under their feet.

A few years ago I was about to hit the road on a stand-up tour so I was doing a few interviews to plug my shows. I was asked by one of Australia's main conservative-leaning newspapers to participate in an interview for a feature in their weekend lift-out about PC culture and its effect on our comedy industry. Without any hesitation I said yes, I was absolutely happy to take part. Why? The same reason I do almost anything. I have tickets to sell and I love money. God damnit I love money. If I weren't so scared of getting a communicable disease, I would eat money. They say it doesn't buy happiness, but it sure does buy a lot of things that look, feel and smell like happiness, so whaddya gonna do?

A time was arranged, I answered my phone at said time and the journalist introduced herself. We took part in some small talk and conversational pleasantries about the weather. Both of us agreeing that sometimes it's too hot but at other times, it can be too cold. Then it was time to get down to the business at hand. I would say within around three minutes it became pretty clear that she was not only completely unaware of my body of work, but also had a fairly basic understanding of the comedy industry at large. We spoke for around three quarters of an hour and I got the feeling I wasn't giving her what she wanted. It was as if this woman had gone into the interview certain that I was going to be of the opinion that PC culture was ruining comedy and that something needed to be done. Somewhere she'd taken the position that the nation was headed towards some cultural dead stop and we comedians were furious about it. Our dialogue got more and more heated as I tried to explain that, yes, you can still say whatever you want these days, it's just that there might be some repercussions. Back and forth we went. Over and over until through breathless anger she roared, 'I mean, don't you think there is . . . it's just like . . . I feel like there is a PC brigade out there trying to ruin the careers of straight white male comedians!'

I tried to answer as diplomatically as possible. 'Oh, I don't think that's true. It's not like there is a secret underground community of minorities working to slowly and systematically destroy the life and works of cisgendered men in the entertainment industry. Hahahahaha. That would be crazy.' I hung up the phone, looked out the window and thought to myself, *We need to be more careful.*

I first joined a local chapter of the PCB in late 2007. I was seventeen and had just begun doing open mic in my hometown of Newcastle. One evening while walking through the venue's car park I was approached by a shadowy figure. 'That was great stuff in there,' she said. How'd you like to serve your country?' She had short, dark hair and wore a long flowing rainbow cape. 'I'm putting together a group of like-minded individuals,' she continued. I would later find out this person was who would become our commander: The Supreme Leader Hannah Gadsby. She was travelling the world to bring together an elite faction of radical queers and people of colour with one goal: the complete destruction and devastation of heterosexual white men.

When I became a member, our organisation was still quite small. Just a few chapters in major cities and their surrounding areas. I trained for a couple of months in the Newcastle office's set-up in the back room of the town's first cafe to serve oat milk. Then when I turned eighteen I was stationed at the headquarters in Sydney, where I worked in what was then called the mailroom. Three years ago, we decided in a meeting that 'mailroom' was too masculine so it's just the 'letter space' now.

Over a decade or so, as we've grown, I've climbed the ranks and worked in several areas of The Brigade. First in Homosexual Recruitment, then internet censorship. For a spell I worked in the casting of crisis actors and I even had a tiny consulting role in a project that would later become known to the public as World Pride. Our work was often slow, arduous, but always rewarding. For years our growing band of merry sexual deviants, racial minorities and people living with a disability set up small mechanisms to tap away at Anglo cis men in politics and the media. The problem was we always came back to the same issue. We kept hitting the same wall. The reason it had all begun. How were we going to ruin stand-up comedy? From the outside it seemed so simple, but it just wasn't. The truth is, white male comedians are like a hydra: every time you cut off one head there's three more ready to tweet #NotAllMen.

We have had our losses, of course. Some downright bungles, to be honest. We probably shouldn't have started Twitter – that was a clear misstep. Several years ago, a mission codenamed 'Honeypot' went pear-shaped when an agent was specially trained to go undercover and create a space in which we could attract and, through clear logic, debunk some of the most dangerous higher-ups of the straight cultural hierarchy. We planted them first in stand-up comedy, then the dizzying world of mixed martial arts. Unfortunately, we hadn't anticipated the pressure this team member could feel from being in there for so long. In the early days of the mission he pleaded we pull him out so he could return to his longtime partner Brendan and their two cats, Betty and Joan. We foolishly resisted and he lost his mind, started smoking cigars indoors and went rogue, starting a podcast called *The Joe Rogan Experience*. It was a learning curve for the whole Brigade. We will never forget how we lost a good agent that day.

It was in a think tank in the summer of 2015 that we had our eureka moment. 'I've got it!' Zoë Coombs Marr shouted. 'We all have to become successful comedians.'

Looking back, it all seemed so straightforward. All we had to do was make it seem as though we were good at comedy, win all the awards and then gaslight the public into thinking racism, sexism and homophobia weren't funny anymore.

By the beginning of 2016 we had a plan. Zoe would win the Melbourne International Comedy Festival's Most Outstanding Show Award (Australia's most illustrious comedy honour), and as an assault on the institution of heteronormative marriage, Zoe and I would get married to each other at a large charity event in aid of queer youth. *That'll get those straight white arseholes*, I thought as we handed over the much-needed cheque. You see, what you need to know is, our work was and never will be about helping people or making them feel included. Sure, it might appear like that from the outside, but no. Our main and only goal is to ruin the lives of men in comedy and their allies. #AllMen. Look, we just have nothing better to do.

AGEING TASTEFULLY

Nothing can make you feel more grown-up than coming to love a food that once made you want to throw up. I reckon I could tie pretty much all my moments of feeling most mature to eating the food I had once so despised. We all can, I guess? Olives, black coffee, the public humiliation of your enemies. They're all flavours you have to develop a palate for, but once you do, there's a touch of superiority to it all. You can look at someone who's younger than you and know in your heart that in some new way, you are better than them. You feel as though you could say, 'Oh, you just don't get it yet' – with the word 'yet' being a real slap in the face to any minor. It's as if you've unlocked a new level of life. Sure, they might understand TikTok and have a genuine concern about the health of the planet, but a stilton blue cheese makes their eyes water, so they are basically a dumb-dumb garbage person.

And the whole superiority complex via cuisine thing doesn't apply solely to one person's tastes, of course. With some food it feels like society as a whole can eventually come around to certain ingredients, which allows us to all feel smug together. It seems to me that from about the 1970s through to the early 2000s, the humble anchovy had a long spell of bad publicity. For decades you couldn't swing a trout without hitting a character in a movie or TV show ordering a pizza and saying something like, 'And no anchovies!' Or, God forbid, if someone did enjoy them, they were treated with the contempt we reserve for people who wish to harm children. People talk about these canned fishy frenemies as if liking or disliking them is equated to their political stance. Not since the brussels sprout went from the grim, over-boiled mush of hospice care wards all the way to being crisped and delicately seasoned by Michelin-starred chefs has an ingredient had such a glow-up. It definitely feels like we are well and truly into the era of anchovies not merely being an ingredient to hide in a sauce or a dressing; it's time for them to come out into the light and have a go at being the main event.

With this in mind, putting out a plate of anchovy toast is one of the easiest and most sure-fire ways to impress dinner guests, I reckon. Like an abstract painting, it's elegant in its simplicity and if people don't care for it, it's the type of classy enough looking dish that any naysayers will assume it's their fault for not appreciating. And they'll pretend to get it anyway. Alternatively, anchovy toast is just a fucking delicious little afternoon snack with big flavours that make you feel like you could be the type of person who has a second home in a charming coastal township. It tastes like approachable luxury. It tastes like linen. It tastes like work–life balance.

Ingredients-wise, you've really gotta let them do the talking here. Don't skimp too much with this one. It's obviously pretty important to use good quality anchovies. John West has earned our respect and his place in the market, but this is not his arena. Go to a classy grocery and treat yourself with some Ortiz or Don Bocarte or something along those lines. The tin should look like great lengths have been taken in order for it to look ye olde.

In this recipe I'm using a garlic confit, but if you're not so inclined, you can cut a peeled clove of garlic in half and rub the exposed sides onto the freshly charred slices of bread. This will leave behind garlic oil that with will soak in and provide a lovely wallop of acidity to cut through the fish.

To be honest, this is the type of simple dish that you can whack all manner of your favourite stuff into and make it your own. Some fresh tomato can add some acidity. Why not try a rich herbed butter? There are a whole bunch of different approaches, but I like 'em pretty basic and let the big ol' sharp tastes have at it. Whatever your preferred style, anchovy toast pairs rather delightfully with almost any kind of aperitif you've got going. I guarantee that when you serve it, people will look more impressed than they should. And if that doesn't make you feel all hoity-toity and grown-up, I don't know, try doing some sort of white-collar crime or something.

ANCHOVY TOAST

– SERVES: FOUR–SIX –

– PREPARATION TIME: FIFTEEN MINUTES –

– COOKING TIME: ABOUT FIVE MINUTES, BUT IT REALLY DEPENDS ON HOW DRUNK YOU ARE –

– INGREDIENTS –

1 medium French shallot, peeled and thinly sliced into rings
about 1 cup nice red wine vinegar, such as merlot
4 cloves confit garlic (recipe below)
1 bunch continental parsley leaves and soft stems, finely chopped
juice 1 lemon
sea salt flakes and freshly ground black pepper
3 tbsp good quality olive oil
1 loaf schmancy sourdough
12 fillets good quality anchovies

– METHOD –

- Pop the shallots into the vinegar and set aside for at least 15 minutes, but longer is better.

- If you're making these for a dinner party and people are arriving, now is the time to prepare yourself a martini or pour a glass of champagne and make an effort to look much, much busier than you actually are. This will ensure people appreciate the rest of the meal later on.

- In a medium mixing bowl, use a fork to mash up the garlic into a kind of lumpy paste. Add the parsley, lemon juice, a pinch of sea salt and pepper and a decent glug of olive oil, then stir it up until the ingredients are all involved with each other.

- To bring it all together, cut some thick slices of bread into 12 fingies, then rub a little oil on each and grill on both sides until they are crisp and slightly charred. Smear some of the garlicky salsa on each piece, put an anchovy fillet on top and decorate with 3 or 4 rings of shallot (up to you but I like quite a bit on there).
- Serve up on a platter and walk around like you're so surprised people like them and as if it was fucking nothing.

GARLIC CONFIT

Oh my god, you're about to have your life changed. Maybe not changed. Altered slightly. If you have any interest in garlic. If you don't, this really won't affect you at all. Maybe even skip this part, actually.

The word 'confit' on a menu sounds like something complicated and dense, but it's deeply easy and sure does render some wildly satisfying results. It just requires using the technique very similar to the personality of the French population as a whole; provide very little warmth and basically ignore until you get the results you want. Hey, it's worked out for them so far.

Just a couple of words on safety, though: you really have to a be a little careful with storing the confit, as I can very much not recommend letting botulism develop in your mix. It has terrible reviews.

Big no from me. So, after you're done cooking, allow the garlic to cool slightly, transfer it to sterilised airtight jars and quick-smart place them in the refrigerator. It's crucial to avoid leaving the garlic confit at room temperature, as this can result in the formation of toxins from bacterial spores, which can increase the risk of botulism. Make sure the cloves are completely covered by the oil and remember, the garlic confit will only remain fresh in the refrigerator for about a fortnight, and in the freezer for up to 3 months.

The confit-ing of garlic makes it soft, tender and more mellow. It's like giving garlic a little Xanax. Mix it into mayo or use some to make dressings. Sometimes I just spread it on charred bread by itself with a little salt. Suddenly you've got this jar of incredibly versatile spreadable bombs of flavour in your fridge.

– PREPARATION TIME: HOWEVER LONG IT TAKES YOU TO PEEL A SHITLOAD OF GARLIC –

– COOKING TIME: TWO HOURS PLUS COOLING –

– INGREDIENTS –

5 bulbs garlic, all cloves peeled (good luck to you)
3 cups decent olive oil
3 sprigs thyme
3 sprigs rosemary

– METHOD –

- Get the oven preheated pretty low to around 120°C fan-forced (140°C conventional).

- Pop the garlic and herbs into a heatproof dish and add the oil. The main thing here is that the garlic has to be completely covered by the oil. Like absolutely submerged.

- Thwack it into the oven and roast for just on two hours. The cloves should be browned and tender. The house is going to smell real nice.

- Remove and allow to cool before transferring to an airtight container or jar. Stored in the fridge, it will keep for two weeks.

UNCLE

If memory serves, being an adolescent is a fucking nightmare. For the obvious and gross bodily reasons of course, but my main recollection of teenagerhood is this feeling of immense powerlessness. Puberty is such a joy because it's the first time you get to feel those first twinges of crippling responsibility but with absolutely zero potential to be able to change any part of our lives. Everyone's always telling you what to do. Telling you how you should know better, but also 'do what I say'. Grow up, but don't get too big for your boots. Go outside, but get inside. Make some friends, but I don't want you hanging out with those people. I didn't have particularly strict parents, quite the opposite, really. They're ceramicists. By nature deeply supportive people who have never tried to stop me following my dreams. But that didn't matter. During puberty you've created this whole paranoid narrative that these parent people are not to be trusted. Their aim is clearly to make you unhappy. You were just going along fine having complete admiration and love for them and then you turn twelve or thirteen and suddenly out of nowhere you look at your guardians and think to yourself, *These people are trying to destroy me. And I'm going to destroy them right back.*

If you're lucky, you have an adult in your family who is a bit more fun than everyone else. Someone who during this vulnerable period gives you the time of day. It could be a grandparent who's always slipping you money in a way that makes you feel like a drug dealer. Maybe your mother has a cousin who keeps dropping stories about your mum's past that you're certain you aren't supposed to know. They could be a twice-divorced aunt who has a slight drinking problem no one is talking about. You know, people who just get it. Not necessarily the black sheep of the family. More . . . the grey sheep. The outsiders on the inside. They are the ones we gravitate towards at any family function in our early teen years because we know they have some editorial. They will have opinions. They will have thoughts about Aunty Marilyn's new job as a sales rep for a vegan aroma diffuser company. Yes, we all know it's a pyramid scheme. No, no one's said anything about it and yes, we will take four.

I don't want to gloat, but I gotta say, when it comes to the cool relative department I think I hit the jackpot. There's a nice cluster of very fun members of my family, but it has to be said, when I was entering adolescence one particular kin rose to the top. When I was thirteen my uncle was a member of seminal early 2000s Aussie alternative rock drug band, Machine Gun Fellatio. If you're unaware of their work, you clearly weren't an Australian uni student in 2002 and may not have even tried any kind of amphetamine. MGF were a band of seven all-singing, all-dancing, uppers-fuelled maniacs. Their live shows were legendary on the Aussie touring circuit. They were known for nudity and lewd acts onstage. Their backstage antics created headlines. They had hit songs like 'Mutha Fukka on a Motorcycle'. Their second album, *Paging Mr Strike*, went platinum, with poppy singles such as 'Rollercoaster' and 'Pussy Town'. They got a lot of attention for their wild behaviour. But as I get older and listen to some of their songs, I'm struck by how beautiful they are. 'Take it Slow', 'The Girl of My Dreams is Giving Me Nightmares' and my personal favourite, 'Unsent Letter', are all soft, artsy ballads about broken hearts. These tracks really hammer home how MGF wasn't just there for shock value. This was an incredibly talented little herd of grey sheep.

The youngest of my mother's siblings by a long shot, Chit Chat Von Loopin Stab (Uncle Glenn to us), seemed to live in a different world to my Newcastle family. A different universe. Sydney. He had moved to the big smoke when he was eighteen and a visit from Glenn was always an event. When I was little and he was in his twenties he'd arrive at the family Christmas deeply hungover, and immediately present all the kids with loud and very messy gifts. Science kits, complicated Lego, musical instruments. It was as if he was trying to ruin our parents' lives and we loved it. He was one of us.

When I was little, maybe nine or ten, when the band played our town I was allowed to go to bed early with the promise that in a few hours' time I would be allowed to get up again because they were all coming round to have showers and a drink after the show. I have such fond memories of my eyes opening to the sight of Christa Hughes, one of the singers who was often nude on stage and someone I'd become so infatuated with she called herself my fairy godmother, belting out 'Diamonds Are a Girl's Best Friend' as she tickled me.

For my eleventh birthday Glenn gave me a framed, signed picture of Christa topless. In the photo she's onstage wearing nothing but a G-string and, of course, fake moustaches taped onto her nipples. She'd signed it with the inscription reading 'Dearest Rhys, Happy legs 11. Lotsa love, Christa'. It was agreed with my parents that, yes, although this is a lovely gift, it is absolutely not the type of thing to take in for show and tell. In fact, don't mention it at school at all. Or to anyone. And maybe hide it when I have friends over. That picture is still one of my most precious possessions and one of the best presents I've ever received, only to be outdone a few years later when he gave me a DVD of the Talking Heads concert film *Stop Making Sense* and in one fell swoop shifted the type of culture I consumed.

A few years after the band dissolved dramatically, Glenn moved with my aunt and my baby cousins back to Newcastle and suddenly he was a much bigger part of my life. Visits were no longer an event but a regular occurrence. I was now sixteen and just a real arsehole. I wasn't wildly off the rails doing meth or anything. Your run-of-the-mill teenager making my parents feel powerless as I screamed things like 'You never listen to me!' but also 'Leave me alone!' And 'You don't understand me!' as well as 'You wouldn't get it!'. I've never been sure if my parents said something to him, but all of a sudden I was over at his house every weekend at his request to help out with random stuff like painting fences, mowing the lawn and moving boxes, but mainly we'd talk. Those conversations that are about nothing but also absolutely everything. We'd talk about what I wanted to do (be a comedian and writer). We'd talk about what he had done and how he'd done it. He explained that, yes, the arts are fun but also incredibly hard and random and they involve a lot of work. We never once spoke about the idea of having a backup. He gave me faith in my plan. He gave me agency.

I should say, he's not dead. Any time someone publicly says something nice about a family member, they are usually dead. No, he's not dead, he just lives in Newcastle – so close.

Now I'm in my thirties, that distrust of my parents has dissolved. I've come out the other side. Now I am an uncle to my young niece and nephew, and my partner and I know we have a responsibility here. I'm not sure they are quite ready for *Stop Making Sense* yet. But maybe an accordion.

HOW TO WRITE YOUR FIRST BOOK: PART III

Well, that deadline is sneaking up fast, isn't it, buddy? By now it is completely normal to have developed an unpleasant, almost menacing tight feeling deep in your chest and at the base of your neck that flares up any time you aren't actively working on the book. Use that. I'm not sure how, but 'using' something like pain is what creatives seem to like saying for some reason. This is a perfect time, instead of actually just knuckling down and working on the task, to spend hours straining and racking your brain about things you could write about that will flow out of your fingers quickly and without a huge amount of lead time. Some sort of easy way out. What if it was some sort of mechanism? A themed device that pops up a few times throughout the book, perhaps? Could there be something every few pages about your experience of writing this fucking thing? Would that be too obviously just a way to fill the pages with words? I mean, it could be nice for your brain to have a little bit of a purge. Just a space for you to pour your little heart out into the laptop and hope people think it's meant to be funny and not in fact a very, very real plea for help and understanding? Would that be good?

Oh! Maybe there's some stuff you wrote years ago you could just drag and drop in? Some stuff that's already seen the light of day and had a good reaction from audiences, so you know it's been tried and tested, too. Find yourself manically trawling through old material and realise you used to have some wildly problematic views and opinions. Delete a huge amount of your Google docs, Twitter account and general social media presence so no one finds these when you die or get booked on a reality show. Oh no, now you're thinking about dying. Well, there goes the afternoon.

A DISH BEST SERVED HOT

Is it just me, or it there not nearly as much revenge going on in adulthood as we were all expecting? It's not as if we were *promised* it but from all the movies I was watching and the stories that were being read to me as a kid, I really thought making people rue the day I was born would be a bigger part of my life. I mean sure, on some level this probably has something to do with the fact that I – like all self-respecting queer children – had always related more to the villains in the stories than the humdrum goody-two-shoed heroes. This is partly because of the pesky, generations-long negative gay coding in popular culture (I'm looking at you, Captain Hook, every single Bond villain and every single character in the *Sex and the City* films), but mostly because of common sense. I guess it's always struck me that in almost every fairytale the so-called evil ones are always somewhere chic and secluded minding their own fucking businesses. Then some rando 'goody' rocks up, somehow completely rips apart the poor villain's life and the latter's retaliation is twisted into some sort of senseless attack. I call bullshit. Imagine you're living in, say, a gingerbread house. You've spent years setting yourself up in the deepest, darkest part of the Deep Dark Forest. You've made a choice to live off-grid. You wouldn't call yourself a tree hugger, but you've certainly been dreaming of a life unplugged for a few years now and it's finally all come together. Maybe there was a time where you wanted to start a family? Perhaps raise a daughter at the top of a tower surrounded by a thicket of poisonous, barbed vines? But life got in the way and you now find yourself retired and single. All in all, you're happy. You garden. You potter around. You make wind chimes out of pieces of scrap wood and daydream that maybe, just maybe, one day they'll be good enough to sell at the general store in town.

Then one afternoon you're sitting in your front room and hear the unmistakable sound of munching coming from outside. So you look through the window and what do you see? A couple of tweens nibbling on the front porch. Yeah, look, I'd be a little hot under the collar, too. I can totally imagine the train of thought that ends with them seasoned, marinated and simmered in a hearty cauldron stew. I mean, who do these little brats think they are? It's already hard enough to maintain a shack made mostly of sugar and flour without these monsters breaking off a few chunks. The lesson baby Rhys took from that tale was: leave people alone and they won't be unwillingly provoked into eating you. It's worked a treat so far.

For years I've heard my mother lament the ways particular characters are villainised in fairytales. She is a stepmother to my sister and has always felt that the way the step community is represented leaves a bit to be desired. Not just in fairytales, either. Broadly speaking, culture seems to have a big problem with step-parents. On a recent rewatch of *The Sound of Music* it suddenly occurred to me how much that film wants you to hate The Baroness Schraeder. Can someone do me a huge favour and enlighten me as to what this woman has done? She turned up to play and when it didn't go in her favour she respectably and classily bowed out. It's not her fault she isn't naturally great with kids or that the man she loves has a thing for virgins who spend way too much time singing in fields. And I'm sorry, but those kids were fucking rude. Frankly if I were one of them and the choice of a mother figure was between someone favouriting a bowl cut who's going to make me do puppet shows well into my late teens, or an aristocratic human lottery ticket in a ballgown who can teach me how to correctly blend a contour during wartime, I know my decision. I wanna be wearing diamonds while drinking expensive schnapps. I do not want to be wearing lederhosen made from the drapes, thank you very much.

I'd imagine that for many step-parents there is so much invisible work being done – just extra little hurdles to jump. It's a delicate balance to keep. Both my parents are very kind, hard-working folk but my mother in particular is one of those people who will go to staggering lengths to make sure people are enjoying themselves. It's something that is very important to her: that everyone is having a nice time.

A trait I've picked up from her is that we are both firm believers in never turning up to someone's house empty handed. The problem is, we both take it to the nth degree. If you say bring snacks, we're bringing groceries. If our job was to supply a salad, well here are three salads and a roast. Oh, we have to bring a main? Well, please enjoy these steaks and your brand-new Jeep Cherokee. This type of behaviour peaked when my sister Ceara and I were kids. Mum had then, and still has now, an incredible ability to be in a constant state of trying to make things memorable and special and nice. It's just down to the way she is, which is wildly and at times terrifyingly generous. On some level, I suppose, many working mums do it. My mother worked a lot when we were little because she needed to. She went back to uni and started a whole new career when I was about four years old. In what is probably a sweeping generalisation, I guess all women in her situation had a completely unwarranted guilt hammered into them about raising children, so now they are desperate for every moment they have with their kids to be remarkable. They want to be nostalgic about something that is happening right now. Mum and Dad both did everything they could to make sure my sister and I were having a nice time. Only when I was older did I find out just how much money we didn't have. But that never stopped them from making sure our family was sorted. There's a story about this time that's almost reached the level of folklore among the Nicholsons. When I was a toddler and my sister would have been about ten, due to circumstances that are frankly none of our business, my parents found themselves down to their last $15. A pretty shit day, I'd imagine. As they sat at the dinner table contemplating their next move, my sister piped up. Completely unaware of the situation, of course, she asked if maybe we could have a treat? And not just any treat. Could we please have the best treat? Could we please get

Magnums? You have to understand that this was the early 1990s. Magnums were the ultimate icy delicacy in pre-millennial Newcastle. They represented a world we weren't a part of. A place with bustling streets and nice restaurants that had real fabric tablecloths where they served rich old ladies who were holding tiny dogs. The Magnum symbolised a better life. Second only perhaps to Viennetta, or the snack of the gods themselves, Ferrero Rocher. So that's exactly what we did. We sat together as a family flat broke, eating rich people ice creams. We had a nice time.

With fancy, expensive trips out of the question, we often leant on visiting family and friends around the country during the school holidays instead. For a few years that meant an annual stop-off to some family friends, Pippa and Steve, at their farm a few hours away. The idea of going to a farm always excited me. For some reason there is a whole lot of farm culture being fed to us at that age. Australian kids all dream we could one day live the rural life. I mean, sure, we have no clue what farms do, but there are animals and you get to wear gumboots with dungarees – the touchstones of an idyllic childhood, in my opinion. Based on *Charlotte's Web* alone, a farm was a magical place where amazing things happen and you just might get to meet a sassy-mouthed, old gay rat.

One such trip we arrived and as the car was unpacked I took in my surroundings and breathed deep, dramatic gulps of air that were thick with that clean mud smell. Yep, this was the life for me. They had donkeys, ducks, a couple of sheep and of course, chickens: a veritable menagerie. I was asked by Pippa if, later on, I would have any interest in going and getting some fresh eggs. In my pre-tween mind she had essentially just told me I was now a farmer, so I was fucking delighted. 'That would be very special and memorable, wouldn't it, Rhys?' my mother said as she unloaded the bags and bags of groceries she'd brought and had in no way whatsoever been told to bring.

For the rest of the afternoon, I was really only interested in getting my mitts on these eggs. I brought it up with Pippa over and over again until finally Mum suggested maybe we could go forth to the henhouse, just the two of us, and leave Pippa alone. Before heading out we were given a warning to watch out for Mr Plymouth. Who was Mr Plymouth?

The enclosure was a large dome where inside about fifteen chickens mindlessly pecked and picked at the ground as if from central casting. They kept their distance as Mum opened the hatch door outwards. I climbed in and wandered around from little box to little box opening each hatch to check for eggs to pop in my adorable, gay-coded little basket. It wasn't the most expansive space, so Mum stayed outside and, I don't know, did whatever parents had to do to keep their minds busy before the invention of smartphones while their kids carried out boring tasks. Stared off into the distance and tried to remember what eight hours of sleep felt like? To be honest, it was all a bit grosser in the enclosure than I was expecting, but who cares – I was a goddamn farmer now. As I approached the last box I heard a bit of a flap and commotion happening way off on a far side of the dome. Choosing to ignore it, I kept to the task at hand. There was some more flapping and then an undeniable shriek. My head darted up and I saw him: Mr Plymouth. The rooster. The literal cock of the walk. In my memory he is at least eight or nine feet tall, has a gun and is not at all pleased I was in there stealing his sister wives' ovum. Somehow tripling in size, he rose up, launched himself straight towards me and began furiously crowing, pecking, clawing and flapping. I cried out and decided being a farmer was no longer my dream career. It seemed I had brought an egg to a cockfight. In one fowl swoop (pardon the pun), Mum dashed into the pen and flung Mr Plymouth to the side while simultaneously grabbing me and transporting me to safety. Dear reader, I was shaken but unharmed. I spent the rest of the holiday feeling very sorry for myself. Even once we'd returned home I couldn't stop thinking about what had happened. Weeks were consumed with reliving in minute detail what my feathery nemesis had done. I even began drawing pictures of terrible things I imagined happening to my assailant – something I'm sure my parents had some big conversations about. What got me was his callousness. After the attack, as Mum had carried me back to Pippa and Steve's house, I'd looked over her shoulder and through the tears in my eyes I saw the rooster deflate to his regular size and just get back to pecking at the ground. How could he be so unaffected after such a vicious assault? On a minor, no less. This rooster was a sociopath and would rue the day I was born.

In retrospect this was a big chicken year for me. A few months later, we were back at school and for some wildly unthought-through reason my teacher had taken his class, a group of preteens, to the local chicken battery farm. Literally the last legal battery farm in Australia. Looking back on it now, I just can't get my head around it. What in God's name were we meant to be learning on this excursion? I don't know. Maybe that public schools need more funding? Honestly I don't remember heaps from that day but a few vignettes stand out to me. Our tour guide was a tall, hollow-cheeked man with wiry salt-and-pepper hair. He had dead eyes and absolutely no idea how to speak to children. The whole expedition felt as though he'd drawn the short straw in the staffroom that morning. Every now and then he'd say something about the chickens and what they did to them at the farm, and one of our teachers would quickly cut in and either translate or clarify something so we would understand. Or in some cases, not understand. At one point a question-and-answer session was held. A sort of *Inside the Farmer's Studio*. One of my peers put her hand up and asked if the chickens were happy there. We all nodded and chattered in agreement that yes, this was a good question. This is what we came here for. Our guide took in a breath and looked into space in a way that made us know this was the first time he'd ever contemplated such a notion. As he was about to answer, my teacher Ms Jacobs cut in and said, 'Yes, I'm sure they are. I think that's enough questions for now. What's next?'

What was next was the most memorable experience I have of that day. The entire class was taken up an open flight of metal stairs on the side of an enormous shed. As the door at the top was slowly creaked opened and we walked in onto a wide, grated platform, we were whacked hard into a sensory overload. The first thing you notice in a vast building housing thousands of unhappy chickens is the sound. It was as if the audio track of every *Real Housewives* reunion, of every season, of every franchise, was layered on top of each other and then Phil Spector mixed it. Then came the smell. Oh, the smell. It was as if the aroma of every portaloo from every music festival of every country were layered on top of on another, and then Phil Spector mixed it.

Life began to feel very warm and dark and suddenly horribly real. Most of the flock were in cages but around the place you could see kind of small, fenced-in platforms where a group of them could 'freely' wander and peck around an incredibly diminutive space. I think in people prisons this is called 'yard time'. Thinking about it now, I can't seem to remember our guide saying anything during this section of the trip. I could easily have been in such a state of disorientation that I didn't hear him, but, frankly, what could he possibly be saying at this point? 'Well, soak this in, kids. This is formative. If you've had a good life, this will hopefully be the most distressing thing your little minds have ever seen.'

The bus ride home was quiet. One thing was clear, I'd be drawing chickens again. We were told we could eat our packed lunches as we headed back. I opened my lunch box to find my grandmother had made one of my favourites: a chicken salad sandwich. Sitting there staring at it, my seven-year-old brain wondered what the chances were that any of the birds I'd seen that day had ever met my sandwich. It all went a bit real and I swapped it with a classmate for a LeSnak and a yoghurt muesli bar. Not really the best exchange, but at least it was a guilt-free meal.

A few months went by and all my chicken-based trauma of the year had dissipated, although I twitched a little when I found out from Dad that in a few weeks we'd be returning to the farm. It was no longer a place of that clean mud smell and patting donkeys. It was now the scene of a crime.

On the drive there, Mum had breezily mentioned that Pippa had something special for me. All afternoon I badgered everyone for more info: What was my surprise? 'Soon,' I was told. When dinnertime finally clocked round, I was near apoplectic – fidgeting and swimming at the table until finally my surprise was revealed. 'Tah-dah!' my someone laughed as a huge rustic-looking pie was placed in the middle of the table. I was confused and could feel everyone's eyes on me.

'This is a very special pie,' Pippa announced.

'Plymouth Pie!' my mother continued, and an eruption of laughter swept over the adults. To this day I am still chasing the feeling I had in that moment. I've not been able to find a drug or any vice at all that can provide the sensation of your greatest enemy literally being served to you on a platter. The night we ate Mr Plymouth remains one of my mother's favourite stories. Apparently I was really, really into dinner that evening. I kept laughing to myself. The pie was delicious. Pippa had seasoned him perfectly. It was respectful. It tasted salty yet sweet. It tasted like revenge.

In Nicholson family folklore, Mr Plymouth will forever be spoken about as a villain, with my mother and I the heroes. The poor guy. He was just there minding his own business and some random goody came in and fucked it all up.

DOPEY-PROOF CLASSIC ROAST CHICKEN

Chickens. You gotta feel for 'em, you know? We could have amorally domesticated and semi-enslaved any number of bird species, but it just so happened to be them. Sorry, guys. I can't help but think the toxic combination of being flightless and having such large, delicious breasts didn't help the situation. It's as if ducks know how tasty they are so they developed a way to at least attempt an escape. Ah well, moving all that horror right over to the side, you have to admit, there are fewer simpler and finer delights than taking a sizzling roast chicken out of the oven. I have been to several dinner parties in my time where the moment this most basic of culinary offerings was placed on the table it was met with uproarious applause. There is something visceral to the experience. My mum taught me how to do a roast. She didn't do much of the cooking in our house but, it must be said, the lady knows how to a crisp up a delectable dead foul.

I roast a chicken pretty much every week, because why not? Heaps of reasons, obviously, but I'm a mostly unemployed, childness show business monster so I could cook a turkey every night of my life if I wanted to.

I have always felt that roasts have a reputation for being hard to pull off. In truth it is far and away one of the easiest things you can do in the kitchen. That's of course a lie, but you know what I mean. It just takes a bit of time. Plus, even the most ethically sourced whole chickens are pretty affordable and it's just bloody nice to have in the fridge to pick at when you get home drunk or to make sandwiches with over a few days. Hey, go crazy, make some stock. God, I sound like a fuckhead but it's true. Sometimes I roast a chicken just so the house smells like it. And if you have the time, don't relegate the roast to your weekend. There is a particularly bougie feeling to roasting chicken on a Tuesday. I recommend it. You won't know yourself.

I reckon the true key to it all is making sure the oven is so hot when you first put it in. It should be absolutely blistering in there. This is going to get that skin crisping early on. You can add whatever herbs you want, really. A chicken is the blank slate of the dead animal world. I just go the classic aromatics because it's what we have on our mostly lifeless balcony herb garden. I find it wildly comforting.

– SERVES: FOUR-ISH –

– PREPARATION TIME: TEN MINUTES –

– COOKING TIME: ABOUT AN HOUR AND A HALF –

– INGREDIENTS –

a 1.6 kg whole chicken
1 bunch of sage
1 bunch of rosemary
1 bunch lemon thyme, plus 15 sprigs extra
1 juicy lemon
3 tbsp salted butter
3 cloves garlic, peeled and finely chopped
3 tbsp olive oil, plus extra
salt and pepper

– METHOD –

- Take the chicken out of the fridge an hour before you plan to start cooking to get it to room temperature. As it's lying there, acclimatising, do your absolute best to delete from your brain the understanding that this wet-winged mass sitting on your bench was once a sentient living thing. Go ahead and preheat the oven to as hot as it'll go (about 240°C fan-forced/260°C conventional).

- Spread a whole bunch of salt and pepper on the walls inside of the cavity (lol) then stuff half the sage, half the rosemary and half the bunch of thyme in there. Roll the lemon between your hand and the bench a few times like it's a rolling pin. I've been told this loosens up the inside, making it juicier. I have no idea if this is true but I've been doing it for too long to change my mind. With a sharp paring knife or a skewer, pretend you're on *Law and Order SVU* and the lemon is a lover who's wronged you. Make a bazillion shallow punctures all over it. This should feel like a crime of passion, but do please be careful. Heave the lemon into the cavity (lol). This is going to feel not quite right. As you tie the legs together with kitchen twine, you may feel some small moments of regret as you remember again that this was once a chicken walking around without a care in the world. Push that feeling down.

- Add the butter, garlic, the leaves from the extra thyme, and a generous glug of oil to a small saucepan. Heat over low–medium, then get it on a low simmer-type of situation, stirring for about 4 minutes until it's all fragrant. Let it cool slightly and steep to develop all the tasty flavours.

- Place the other half of the herbs in a little pile in a roasting tin and drizzle with oil. This will look like a cute little nest. The nest will remind you again this is a bird that is no longer alive. Fucking hell.

- Place the chicken on the nest and then pour the butter and garlic mixture over the top. Use your fingies to get all up in there. Rub it. Get the butter into every nook and/or cranny. Season with salt and pepper over the top.

- Whack it in the oven and immediately turn the temperature down to 200°C fan-forced (220°C conventional). Roast for about an hour and fifteen minutes. I usually baste it a couple of times and jam a meat thermometer into the thickest part of the breast near the thigh to see how it's going. Be careful it isn't touching bone though – we don't care how hot the bone is. It can give an incorrect reading and then the next thing you know you're feeding your family poisonous chicken and they all die so suddenly it's off to jail because you couldn't prove it was an accident. You want it to have an internal temp of 75°C so you don't kill people.

- Remove her from the oven, cover with foil and leave to have a nap for 15 minutes. Before I carve it up I will usually sit the chicken up and let the surprisingly huge amount of scorching hot juices come pouring of out the cavity (snigger) into the tin. The lemon has exploded in there so what you're witnessing is some fucking delicious citrusy, herby, chicken fat liquid gushing out that is either great as a base for a gravy if you're making one, or perfect to drizzle as is over the carved white meat.

- Carve it up, baby.

RHYS NICHOLSON

JUST ROAST POTATOES, OKAY?

There are a bazillion side pieces you can have sitting next to your perfect roast chicken and, hey, go crazy! Broccolini is really having a strong few years. But I don't think you should be able to look yourself in the face in the morning unless you can prepare some half-decent roast potatoes.

Look, this is serious and I am not fucking around here. If someone in your life is ever, like, 'I don't know, I guess I'm just not really into roast potatoes,' it's time to get them down to the ol' brain doctor for a bit of an MRI scan because something very off is definitely going on in there. None of this skin-on boiled with some butter and salt and bullshit. We aren't at war, we're aiming for crunchy to the touch – almost like crackling – then steaming and fluffy on the inside. The kind of roast potatoes that people will return to for seconds for when there is still some of the main meal left.

When I was growing up, the roast potato was a sacred thing in my family, something to be respected but also something over which great battles were fought. Both my parents make such good potatoes that my sister and I would brawl over the last few. Over the years this behaviour forced my father to double the quantity of potatoes he bought each week, as if our family were involved in some sort of study to see how much starch the human body can actually consume and what the results are.

This is not a complicated recipe because I personally don't think roast potatoes should be. None of these wild ten-times-cooked malarkey. Let's leave that to the professionals. But it is important to not overcrowd your baking tray, because when the potatoes touch each other, heat from them is trapped underneath and creates steam – and soggy food won't crisp up. Leaving space between the potatoes will allow the Maillard reaction that comes from the heating of amino acids, found in protein and sugar, to give your browned food its desirable flavour.

– SERVES: ABOUT FOUR –

– PREPARATION TIME: TEN MINUTES –

– COOKING TIME: ABOUT AN HOUR AND A HALF –

– INGREDIENTS –

1 kg waxy potatoes (e.g. Dutch cream)

sea salt

decent olive oil

1 tbsp fresh rosemary leaves

1 tbsp fresh thyme leaves

2 cloves garlic, peeled and super finely chopped

– METHOD –

- Preheat your oven to 200°C fan-forced (220°C conventional).

- Peel the potatoes and cut them into 4–5 cm chunks. Pop them in a saucepan and cover with just enough cold water to have them all submerged and then add a few pinches of salt. Bring to boil on a high heat and as soon as it's on a rolling boil reduce the heat to medium so it's just on a simmer. Keep it simmering for about 3 minutes.

- As this is happening, pour out a few glugs of olive oil onto a large rimmed (lol) baking tray (with a lipped edge). Not loads, but enough to cover the surface of the tray and have it pool slightly. Add the herbs and garlic to the tray and move them around so the oil is evenly spread. Pop the tray in the oven for a few minutes until it's hot, hot, hot.

- When the potatoes are finished parboiling, drain them thoroughly in a colander and then shake them around in there until their surfaces are roughed up.

- Carefully take the tray of hot oil out of the oven and even more carefully place the potatoes onto it. Turn them around a few times until they are all coated in the shiny, herby, garlicky oil. They should be in a single layer and as spread out as possible. This is to make sure the tiny tato babies have enough space to crisp up as they drown in hot oil. Pop them in the oven and cook for about 20 minutes, then remove and turn them over, return them to the oven for another 20 minutes, then turn once more and roast some more until they look completely golden, crispy and slightly puffed up (about another 20 minutes, but keep an eye on them).

- Sprinkle with salt and serve immediately alongside your roast chicken.

COMEDY LAND

Sometimes I get booked to do storytelling shows. I quite like doing them because usually I'll just do a bit of stand-up, but at a slightly slower pace to make it seem more sentimental. That's all comedy is, really. Sad things said slightly faster than you usually would. I'd been asked to write and perform a little piece for a show at a trendy venue in a trendy suburb of trendy Melbourne. Everyone was telling their story about a time they wished they'd not left something unsaid. I like the audience at this type of show – a late-afternoon-early-evening artsy type of crowd. A lot of unmarried couples in their sixties who wear enormous glasses with brightly coloured frames. The old men are dressed like French sailors and the women wear felted brooches and look like that one high school art teacher who'd let you swear in her class.

The week before, I sat down to write my piece. What is a moment in my life I really wish I had said something? As I convened at my laptop with an empty page and a blinking cursor in front of me, my first thought was, *Well, I wish I'd said no to doing this gig.* Not just this gig.

Any gig, really. I struggled to think of something, anything. For a few days. Not because I'm the person who doesn't leave anything unsaid. Far and away from it. I cannot deal with confrontation. Even the slightest notion of conflict sends me into a retreat. Last year I bumped into a doorframe and instinctively apologised. I apologise for everything, even when I don't mean it. It's a nervous twitch. Every single night I lie in bed, shut my eyes and my brain plays a highlights reel of its favourite show, *My Regrets*. It doesn't rate well, but it's a critical darling. It's not solely confrontation I have a problem with, though. Just anything that could veer on making someone I'm talking to bored or uncomfortable. This can mean I regularly make what could be described as somewhat irrational decisions. Not too long ago I came to terms with the fact that I am a non-binary person, and the idea of having to tell everyone that was a nightmare. It's got nothing to do with the fact I'm non-binary itself – I am proudly so, and frankly a little excited about it. But the idea of telling absolutely every single person I know, one by one, when I've already come out as gay and I'm thirty-two and what do these people want from me? Ergh. Seems like a lot of work. So I made the completely logical decision to painstakingly write a show about it, *Rhys! Rhys! Rhys!*, toured it for more than a year and just kind of hoped it was out there enough for everyone to hear about.

The problem is, if my Wikipedia page is to be believed, I am a stand-up comedian. This means, by definition, I am a liar and thief. To work in comedy is to be a vulture. Always picking and pecking at the lives of our family, friends and strangers so we can turn them into easily consumable content for a largely faceless audience and feel the warmth of laughter to replace the hugs we did not get as children. It's simple. Comedians lie. That's the job. It's mostly small exaggerations or melding two stories together. Saying something happened to us when it actually happened to a friend. Or maybe if something embarrassing happened to us, we say it happened to a friend. I would say the aim is to portray ourselves, in every situation, as the winner. As a strong force for truth. Bullies always get their deserved comeuppance when the tale is told by a comedian.

What's strange is, if you do this for long enough you actually start to remember the lies as if they're real. It's a kind of comedy dementia. I don't have to exist in the real world; I can be in comedy land. I live in a place where I've never left anything unsaid. Where I'm forever articulate and witty, dapperly dressed and always have the last word. I squash every argument with an acerbic aside. It's a dream for me but must be a true hellscape for those directly around me. Kyran is constantly having to remind me on the way home from dinner parties that yet again I have presented a joke as fact and no, during the lockdowns we did not, in a desperate attempt at fitness, try and have sex under a weighted blanket. Please stop telling people that.

There is a story in a show I toured once that goes like this: I got mugged last year. I've been mugged a whole bunch of times. I just keep getting mugged. There's something about me. I scream, 'Mug me!' Which I should stop doing. Because I keep getting mugged.

I was doing some work in New Zealand. I tell you what, New Zealand is a perfect country. If you haven't been, you gotta go to New Zealand. On a side note, this is how perfect a country it is. A few years ago I had done some shows in Auckland and I had a 6 am flight back home. On my way to the airport I realised I had lost my passport. This had never happened to me. I'm not the type of person to let something like this happen to me. I didn't know what to do so I just went to the check-in desk and said, 'I have lost my passport and I need to get home.' The Kiwi at the counter seemed completely not worried in the slightest. His exact words were, 'No worries, bro. Let's call Canberra.' Then we went into a little room where he proceeded to call Canberra, I suppose. They had a 15-minute coded conversation and when he hung up he told me, 'Well, they said it's up to us . . . so I reckon just go.' A perfect country.

But back to New Zealand last year. I'd finished some TV work and literally the next day Australia closed its borders and I was trapped. I had no idea when I was going home or even how. And look, I realise thousands of people have been through something like this in the last few years, but I am a minor celebrity judge on a reality show, so my pain matters more. I had been away for months. I missed my partner. I missed my house. I just wanted to go home. The day after the borders closed I was on the phone to Kyran, walking down Queens Street, one of Auckland's main drags. I had my purse under my arm and I was just raging. Kyran was raging. Not at each other, just at the situation. The feeling we've all had of existential fury that we can't actually pin on anyone. As I was walking I suddenly felt a tug at the purse and I swung around and standing there was this guy. And he looked like someone had made a mugger on The Sims. Because I have been mugged so much I knew straight away what was happening and I said down the phone, 'Kyran, I'm being mugged,' which made him freak out. And now me and my assailant were just standing there. I don't know how but there was something about him that made me realise this was his first mugging. I'm an old hat at this so my next thought was: *Why do I have to do this with the work experience kid?*

I made a look at him as if to say: 'WELL.' He bucked himself up and said, 'Hey, man, give me your purse.' There was a little look in his eye like, 'Is that a purse?' Then something just snapped in my brain. I have a lot of anger inside of me, anger I usually push down. (I'm either making a diamond or a tumour.) I got real close to him and I said, 'Hey! Fuck you! I am not a man!' And he legged it. That's what happened in comedy land: I was strong, outspoken and demanded someone know they had misgendered me. I won.

Almost everything in that story is true. I did get mugged by a new mugger, I did shout fuck you but I did not say I am not a man. That's what I wish I'd said. That's what I wish I was saying every day. In the real world I continue to struggle to articulate how I feel about my own gender. It can at times be incredibly overwhelming.

What actually happened in the real world is that I did get in close and say, fuck you, then unfortunately I slipped on a step, hit the ground and got a little bit winded. As I lay there, writhing on the cold kiwi concrete, I think it was all a bit too much for him and he legged it. Nobody won.

I think about him sometimes. Poor guy. He would have to have gone home that night to his little criminal house. I imagine him looking in the bathroom mirror and saying to himself, 'Tomorrow will be better. You just have to get in there, grab the purse and go. And don't misgender them, 'cos they don't like that.' I also wonder what his version of the story is? What does he tell his friends happened? I hope he won.

A FEW BAD EGGS

As we've discussed before, albeit in a rather one-sided conversation, there is a lovely feeling of merit to getting older and beginning to enjoy the foods you had disdain for throughout childhood. To being a grown-up, as I like to think of it. There's also something quite liberating about taking control of your own culinary narrative by turning your back on some of the most basic parts of the food world you no longer need to stand by. The meals, or even just ingredients, you've had to endure your whole life purely because everyone told you they're good. For me, this means eggs. I'm done with 'em. It's not an allergy thing or some grand repositioning of my moral compass; it's got nothing to do with the ethics of it all. Sure, it probably should, I guess. Only just this second as I'm thinking about it am I beginning to feel a little unnerved by how comfortable I am with the fact that a not insignificant part of the human diet is just unfertilised ovum of a flightless bird we've mass domesticated. It's sounds stranger and stranger the longer you let you brain sit on it, actually.

Let's move on quickly because if we stop to mention each and every single time the human race has done some bizarre thing that seems normal but is actually monstrous, this will quickly become much less of a silly comedy book and more of a harrowing, never-ending list on an Excel spreadsheet about why we should probably stop being a species at all. Anyways, long story short, I just don't love the texture of eggs, and I'm not staying quiet about it any longer. Never again will I sit down at breakfast to pretend I'm going to enjoy a pile of hot, scrambled, yellow mess or the downright unnatural consistency of a poached egg. Nothing should be able to somehow be both soggy and dry – nothing! It's not right. When I first started being more open about my new eggless life (living in eggsile), I was gobsmacked, and a tiny bit elated, by the reaction of panic and fury from the people around me. Once, I was with a very close friend at a douchey cafe known for their apparently very impressive omelette. When I ordered a BLT and mentioned I wasn't messing around with eggs anymore, she reacted as if I'd just asked the waitress to please bring the chef out so I might spit directly into their mouth and pour my iced coffee down the front of their pants. Who knew people cared so much about fucking eggs?

I kept finding myself in these strange, hushed arguments at brunch places with my loved ones as they quizzed me and I'd have to breathlessly explain that I still respect eggs, I just think of them more as a character actor who's great in a supporting role but to me, no longer leading-lady material. They're undeniably an important binding force in some incredible creations, but it feels strange to see them by themself. They're the Ringo of the food pyramid, if you will.

It can be hard to describe where the line is. For me, the tipping point and the main perpetrator of darkness has to be the quiche. We need to wake up to ourselves as a society and to stop pretending quiche is in any way whatsoever an acceptable foodstuff for consumption. It's true, the French have given us so much to be thankful for. Braille, hot air balloons, children who smoke – their cultural gifts to the world are almost unsurpassed. But I just can't forgive them for being single-handedly responsible for every white lady in her sixties who, when asked to bring a plate to a barbecue, turns up with a cold, shallow bucket of pastry that looks and feels like someone has baked some sick then popped it in the fridge overnight.

When I first started getting more into cooking, one of the first things I ever baked was a citron tart. A rather wild choice in retrospect, considering I could have started off with something easier like biscuits or one of those microwaved mug brownies unbalanced people make on TikTok. A citron tart is Kyran's favourite dessert and it was early enough in our relationship that I was still trying to simultaneously impress him and distract him from my occasionally irrational behaviour when I baked my debut effort. Not long before, the idea of baking anything more complicated than one of those supermarket pre-made tubes of cookie dough you see teenagers and divorced dads holding at the check-out felt absolutely impossible. The very concept that I could mix a bunch stuff together in a bowl to form a crude slop, then whack it into the oven for a bit, only to return and find out a while later it had, through some unknown magic, turned into something delicate, textured and delicious, seemed like an unobtainable fantasy. This was something that always ended up making people cry in TV cooking competitions. I mean, *pastry*. Can we talk about pastry? People are just fucking terrified of pastry. I remember reading a recipe for homemade puff pastry many years ago and it shook me to my core. The process looked as though it was endless. The sheer amount of time spent monitoring it, resting it, moving it and rubbing it. The whole escapade sounded more like the care instructions for an elderly, deaf, severely skittish rescue greyhound. Cooking anything with a lot of complicated steps had always seemed so daunting, but over the last few years I actually find myself leaning into it more than following quicker recipes. To me, a no-frills lemon tart is a perfect gateway drug into the heavier end of homemade baked goods. Honestly, making a very basic shortcrust isn't hard at all if you follow the process and, let me tell you, being able to answer 'yes' to the question 'Did you make the pastry?' is literally one of life's sweetest victories. It's as if you've just won a massive fight even though the person asking actually has no idea they are even in an argument. But rest assured, you just won it. It's a similar sensation to sliding a coaster under someone's glass in your own home. As if to say, 'We have nice things here and you wouldn't understand.'

If you're brand new to baking, the task of rolling out the whole slab of pie dough and transferring it to the tin without both the dough and your life falling apart can seem stressful and like, a lot. First of all, pull yourself together. It's only fucking flour and butter, but I get what you mean. Don't be a hero. I usually don't bother and instead, before I pop it in the fridge, I shape the dough into a kind of oblong rather than a disk. You never expect to hear or see the word oblong anymore, but there it is. After it's chilled, instead of rolling it out, cut the oblong into 1.5ish cm strips, then with a little flour on your fingies press the dough pieces against the sides and bottom of the tin. I like to use a small glass or measuring cup to help press it into the sides evenly.

I've made this so many times and it's a big mixture of a few different recipes I've followed over the years. Rather frustratingly, the first time I ever made it, I absolutely nailed it and ever since have fucked it up in some small way without fail. I've been chasing that first-time high for over a decade. Luckily, this is, once again, one of those things that even if it's a bit scrappy, it's still good. Just call it rustic. If people want to complain, see if they can make one better. Dare them. Destroy another relationship. Good riddance, I say. I bet they like quiche and use store-bought shortcrust anyway.

SWEET LEMON QUICHE (BAKED CITRON TART)

– SERVES: ONE–SIX –

– PREPARATION TIME: TWENTY-FIVE MINUTES –

– COOKING TIME: AN HOUR, PLUS COOLING –

– INGREDIENTS –

Sweet almondy shortcrust pastry

500 g plain flour, plus extra for dusting

140 g icing sugar

½ cup flaked almonds, toasted
250 g unsalted butter, cubed
4 egg yolks

Filling

150 ml crème fraîche
5 eggs
140 g caster sugar
juice 3 largish lemons (around 100 ml), plus 2½ tbsp lemon zest

icing sugar, to serve
raspberries, to serve (optional)

– METHOD –

- Whack the flour, sugar, almonds and butter into the bowl of a food processor with the blade attachment and get it going until it's blended into something similar to damp sawdust. Yummy.
- With blades still going, add the egg yolks and keep whizzing until it looks like something similar to damp sawdust that has just had egg yolks added to it. About a minute.
- Now pour in 1–2 tablespoons cold water and keep it going until it comes together into something that looks similar to something that used to look like sawdust with egg yolks in it. Dough? It should look like a dough.

- Sprinkle a little flour on the counter and place the dough onto it, flour your hands and bring it all together into a ball then squash it down a little into a disk and then a flat kind of oblong. Split in two and save half for another time. (It can be frozen for up to a month when wrapped in plastic wrap.) Wrap today's little dough boy in plastic wrap and refrigerate for about an hour.

- Preheat the oven to 180°C fan-forced (200°C conventional).

- Lightly grease a 22 cm loose-bottomed (my nickname in high school) round fluted tart tin. Grab your dough out of the fridge, cut it into 2 cm strips and arrange them evenly around the bottom and sides of the tin. The idea isn't to cover completely, just evenly, because now using your fingies and a cold round glass or metal measuring cup dusted with a little flour, press the dough down and around until it's uniformly covered the entire inside of the tin. It's good if there's a little overhang around the edges. Pop it in the freezer for 10 minutes so it firms up again. Use a sharp knife to trim the edges and prick the base with a fork. Keep the extra dough because you may soon need it. Refrigerate for 30 minutes.

- Line the pastry case with baking paper and fill with rice, dry beans or proper baking weights if she's fancy. Bake for 15 minutes, remove the paper and whatever you used to weigh it down and bake for a further 10 minutes or until the pastry is light golden. If there's any crack, calm down. Grab some of that extra raw dough and spackle it up.

- Remove from the oven and set aside, keeping it in the tin. Reduce oven temperature to 140°C fan-forced (160°C conventional).

- To make the lemon filling, place all the ingredients, except the zest, into a bowl and whisk to combine. Strain the mixture through a sieve into a clean bowl. Transfer the tart to a baking tray and carefully pour the filling into the tart shell. Evenly sprinkle the zest over the top.

- Bake for 30–35 minutes or until just set. There should still be quite a bit of wobble in the centre but you don't want it to be liquidy. Turn off the oven and open the door to allow the tart to start cooling. Allow it to cool completely before removing it from the tin, then serve either at room temperature or chilled. Dust with icing sugar and if you wanna go crazy, I don't know, whack some raspberries on there. Why not, you know? This is your life.

PRETEND PROBLEMS

If you were to ask an artist, of any kind, what their job is, they will no doubt get lost in a wordy tangent about how all creative work aims to challenge the norms we hold dear as a society in the hope of helping to shape that society. Even in just some small way. This is, of course, bullshit. What we're actually trying to do is monetise something that comes naturally to us while making it look very, very hard. That's the main thing about making art. It must look very difficult or it's not worth doing or telling anyone about. Just ask the people who've been around me while I've been putting together this book of light-hearted yet incisive and culturally penetrating essays. From the way I was talking you'd think I was working on a sequel to *Ulysses* and then on my days off having a whack at curing bone cancer. Creative types are simply gluttons for punishment, as long as we can do it publicly.

In August 2018 I was where I basically always am at that time of year, in Scotland doing the Edinburgh Fringe Festival. The Fringe is the world's largest arts festival, boasting more than three thousand separate shows with millions of tickets sold over the four long weeks of its duration. It's a special time of year when the world descends upon this beautiful old city to witness the hundreds and thousands of performers of all styles stage their wares while also having very public, emotional breakdowns. I've been doing shows there every year for almost a decade and it never ceases to amaze me just how much of a slog it is. It's fucked-up. Well and truly fucked-up. But also stunning and remarkable and magnificent. But mostly fucked-up. For us, the pain-yearning artistic community, we are like little piggies in shit. The problem is that it's all way too big. The idea you could ever truly make a splash in such a wide, thick pool of talent is near impossible, so you can spend year after year performing to empty rooms after squandering hours of each day handing out flyers to your own show in the rain to drunk Europeans.

And I tell you what, they do *not* want your flyer, because they've already got tickets to see a burlesque-circus-cabaret extravaganza where for 55 minutes some hungover clown who has a BO problem and calls himself a feminist for the wrong reasons is going to slowly push a large ball across the stage as a topless lady in the corner does a cover of 'Creep' on an accordion. When we return to our friends and family afterwards, we tell stories about performing in Edinburgh as if we had been to war. On meeting anyone else who's done it, all we can offer is a sympathetic look of recognition. We were there too. We have the sclerosis of the liver, the mammoth carbon footprint and the chasm of self-loathing to prove it. It is financially ruinous for most, and mentally catastrophic for all. Yet we can't stop going. Like that rush of endorphins that washes through a new mother straight after the birth of her child to make her feel okay about the fiasco she just went through, on 1 September we performing artistes are new again. There are ludicrous conversations between contemporary dancers, acrobats, actors and comics as if these twenty-five nights of performance are our Gallipoli. Then we discuss which venue we want to do next year and what our poster might look like. The Edinburgh Fringe has this incredible ability to fill any performer with wonder and awe while at the same time bringing on an intense sensation that you are unsafe and in some unknown way being interfered with. It's a lot like watching a close-up magician for a month. In some ways literally.

One night at around 1 am, sometime during the third week of the festival, I was waddling home in the ever-present sprinkle of Scottish rain and feeling in a bit of a slump. Nothing too serious, just a bit grumpy. That year I was performing in a small room within the venue known as 'Cowgate'. While the name Cowgate suggests some sort of conspiracy by the government to hide state secrets about livestock, what it is in reality is a maze of teeny tiny performance spaces carved into the stone of a bridge built sometime in the 1700s. I'm sure you can imagine they are stunning rooms with very good ventilation. No. There are blazing house fires with more fresh air. Let me be clear: this is not a judgement on the facilities Cowgate provides. This is stock standard for the Fringe and in fact I've actually been very lucky with the places I've taken my little comedy concerts to. With almost every inch of the city having been converted into a stage, I was lucky to have seats, let alone lights and a microphone. I once saw a dear friend do their show in a clay yurt built on the side of the road. The audience sat cross legged on the floor while he performed a phenomenal hour of stand up, and I couldn't help but wonder the whole time if he was about to bring on the shaman to guide us through the ayahuasca ceremony I must have forgotten I'd booked myself into. Is this what show business had promised us – the chance to ply our trade in a sweaty, windowless kiln and perform so close to the audience that we could smell the dinner on their breath?

My show throughout the 2018 season was going well enough, I suppose, but my moodiness was the result of an accumulation of things. Earlier that day while flyering, I'd watched an old man accept the flyer from my hand, look me up and down, narrow his eyes and ask, 'Is this you?' When I responded in the affirmative, he wandered down the street and I soon spied him as he popped the picture of my face directly into a bin. Goooood. At least he wasn't a litterbug, I suppose. I had done my best to shake off that feeling but then hours later during the show itself I'd had full view of a drunk young woman in the audience fall into a deep sleep and stay there for the remainder of the hour. And boy was she comfortable – didn't even stir for a moment. I was jealous. I tried to shake it off, but you have to admit, it's hard not to view one person binning my face and another taking a nap during my offer to the art form a little personally.

So after the show I told myself I deserved a little treat. This is how I get through anything even slightly close to a slog: exercise, hitting a deadline, remembering my partner has feelings. All come with a little self-endowed reward to give me some pep. Something I've done for years during long festival runs is every night just before my show I buy a Snickers (objectively the best chocolate bar) and place it in my pocket. Then, without fail, during the show I will completely forget it exists and as I trudge out of the venue I'll slide a hand into my pocket and lo and behold, there's a little gift from my ol' pal Past Rhys. But given my mood that night, a delicious Snickers (that I would happily continue to write about if there was perhaps some sort of arrangement) wasn't going to cut it. I needed something carb loaded. I needed something that glistened with animal fat. I needed something Scottish.

I love the cuisine of bonnie Scotland dearly and without any shame. While much of the food world has in recent years veered towards lighter, fresher fare with bright hues of green and primary colours in their dishes, the Scots have really stuck to their guns by choosing to remain in a culinary space with a colour palette closer to the leather goods section of a department store. Oh and the textures! Things are either very, very crisp or damn near slop. It's a tactile spectrum with very little middle ground. I'm not saying it's not creative. Far from it. The fish and chip mongers in that country are in particular true pioneers of the art form. They'd deep fry and eat a doorknob if they could. And we would eat it, happily. I'm sure it'd be delicious with something poured over it like the mysterious Brown Sauce that's available in all the chip shops there. The only thing the locals say about it is how it's great on chips. 'Yes,' I agree, because it is, 'But what's *in* it?' No one knows. Perhaps it's for the best I don't find out so I can continue to enjoy Brown Sauce like I'm some witless background character in *Sweeney Todd*.

In my time at the Fringe I have made it my mission to try as many local delights as humanly possible, from the clichéd haggis to the viscerally named cullen skink and even chicken tikka masala (look it up). By about the third week of August every year my small intestine has begun to resemble the inside of Noah's ark and I'm no longer in charge of when or where I will very suddenly need a bathroom with floor-to-ceiling doors. As I was heading home, while thinking it all over and having my gloominess in mind, I decided the only thing to feed my carbs lust that night would be a modest portion of hot chips and for after, that delicacy of the people – a deep-fried Mars bar to be enjoyed following the smoking of my nightly nigh-nighs medicine.

While I'd been onstage that evening I had a missed call from my agent, Kat, in Australia, that was followed up with a text from her simply reading, 'Call me as soon as you can.' When you receive a message like that in the middle of the night from another country by the person in charge of your money, your mind doesn't leap to good news. I automatically figured someone had found those deeply problematic tweets from when I was nineteen. Maybe I was being cancelled. *Ah well,* I thought. *I've had a good run. Maybe I can have a little rest.*

Unfortunately on this occasion I wasn't cancelled. The call was to check my interest in an offer that had come through from a large production company known for making shiny big-budget TV shows. They wondered if I would potentially be interested in being booked as a member in the cast of a celebrity competition reality show. You know the one. For about forty-five minutes we spoke down the line about the deal and what it would involve. I've never been one to watch these types of shows. Don't get me wrong, I've never thought I was above doing them. Lord, no – not in the slightest. Give me a few more years and I'll be saying yes to each and every one of them. I'd go on a show called *Rhys Nicholson Fights a Bear While all Their Exes Watch* if it was for the right price. I think I've just always preferred the talent-based shows, especially the ones from twentyish years ago when it all seemed a bit more innocent: *Idol*, *So You Think You Can Dance*, *Bake Off*. It feels as though from 2003 until about 2012 you couldn't turn on the TV without seeing some random being ripped from obscurity and having their lives change by becoming a household name and then being gaffer taped to a million-year-long record contract. I eat that shit up. And give me a sob-story while you're at it. Show me a single-income orphan battling a terminal illness with a golden set of pipes and a couple of tappin' shoes that won't quit and I am locked and loaded.

The 'celebrity' ones, on the other hand, are a bit of a different story. If I were to say yes, in around six months I would be flown to a remote and exotic country to join a group of people with wildly varied levels of notoriety where we'd be pitted against each other as each of us scratched and clawed our way through a series of challenges, each more embarrassing than the last, all in the name of charity. If I said no . . . well, I was strongly urged not to say no. As it was sold to me, if I was to do well on a show like this (whatever 'doing well' means), not only would I be given quite a silly amount of money, but I'd also be a tiny bit famous. Ascending the fame ladder even a small amount could lead to more ticket sales of my shows, bigger opportunities and maybe even something like a book. Who knows. I loved the irony of having to go on a show for celebrities to become one in the first place. Sure, I might have to eat some strange parts of animals and get bitten by a snake in front of one of the Daddo brothers, but afterwards I would have a bit more clout and could be more selective with the work I was doing, instead of just saying yes to whatever came up.

Undeniably, being a bit famous would be hugely helpful. A greasing of the wheels. I knew it then and I know it now because at the time of writing this, at this very moment, I am the tiniest bit famous. Not wildly so. An al dente amount. And I gotta say, I fucking love it. I really do. It's just the best. You're not meant to say that, I know. As creative types we're supposed to pretend we didn't expect it to happen. As if we had no idea this was even a possibility. 'Oh I just do it for the art,' we creative types with a modicum of fame say to a dinner party of friends in their five-bedroom country homes, taking a break from the bustle of the inner-city pad. Oh okay, yeah, of course. It's just for the love of the work. Not the money and added perks. And I go on Pornhub to read the comments. Yet, it can't be denied, even with my low level of renown it's not always ideal. There is sometimes an odd feeling of ownership strangers have over me when we meet in person. I'm not always allowed personal space and there are definitely parts of the internet I will never look at again for fear of reading the deeply troubling things faceless avatars have said about me and the things they would like to happen to me. That being said, there are three nice restaurants in Melbourne that will give me a table any time I like, and Selma Blair follows me on Instagram. So it all kind of evens things out.

The idea of going on a reality show was never the direction I thought I'd be going in career-wise, but who was I to turn it down? I was a semi-professional stand-up comedian who also seemed to be moonlighting as a sleep therapist for the female youth of Scotland. 'Ergh,' I said down the line to Kat. 'Will I have to humiliate myself and eat gross stuff?' I thought about my flyer in the garbage and looked down at the styrofoam container of chips and Scottish mystery sauce. Yes. I said yes.

By early September, with my season in Edinburgh over I was back home and had signed the contracts tying me with very little escape to the TV show. It was almost five months until I'd be heading off into the wilderness and what now needed to happen was a series of medical exams, painful immunisations for rabies and malaria, plus a psychological test that was done via webcam. I presume for insurance reasons they wanted to be certain I was at least vaguely healthy so my heart wouldn't explode at the top of a ropes course and there wasn't the risk I was going to be losing my mind in there. And if I did have a psychotic break, it could be something juicy and good for ratings, like an admission of some past trauma, or maybe I try to open mouth kiss the dangerous right-wing media commentator they always seem to have on these programs.

Something that had really been hammered into me was the importance of keeping it all secret. They weren't kidding around. If the production got even a whiff that I'd been shooting my mouth off about my participation ahead of the first episode, they could sue me for breach of contract. I allowed myself one exception and told a close friend, partly for my own mental health to get it off my chest, but mostly knowing that if the show wanted to sue me, well, good luck with that. Had they wanted to take me for all I was worth, I hoped they could enjoy owning my thousands of dollars of credit card debt, my decades-long collection of *Vanity Fair* magazines and the Sega Mega Drive I don't know how to plug into the TV. Have at it, champs. I had also chosen my pal as my one vessel because she had been on one of these shows before and I knew I could squeeze some advice out of her. We went out for dinner and I grilled her on how I should prepare. It felt fun to be getting secret in such a public place, as if we were in a spy novel.

Firstly, speaking practically, she urged me to gain some extra weight. They apparently feed you little more than a handful of rice each day and my body would need something to chow down on before it inevitably got to work on atrophying my brain so I'd start to admit all my secrets on camera. I ordered another entree and she continued. What she was most clear about was how I should never, and she meant never ever, tell a single person on the production about any fears or phobias I might have. 'Especially not the psych they have hired. They will 100 per cent use that on the show,' she said. They'll say they won't, but the moment you tell them you're scared of heights and snakes they'll have you over a ravine wearing a harness made out of live asps.' I took this advice seriously and when asked, I told the psych what I was most scared of in the world was success, shoulder rubs and seeing nudes of the cast of the hit CW network's gritty reboot of *Archie*, *Riverdale*.

I suppose it was around mid-January and just a couple of weeks until I jetted off into the unknown. Over the past months I had kept my mouth mostly shut, all the while doing my best to prepare myself for what was coming. I'd also really started to lean into the idea of people in this part of the biz. *Once I'm famous maybe I won't even have to do stand-up anymore? I might not have to. I'll get one of those famous people jobs. Maybe I could host one of those terrible podcasts where a bunch of white people sit around talking about how the atrocities of the world make them feel sad before doing unboxing videos of free shit?* When I wasn't daydreaming about my upcoming new life, I was checking I was prepared. Apart from the tests and injections, I had quietly rescheduled my upcoming tour, meaning the reality show was now my only income for the next six months. *Shouldn't be a problem; I'll be drowning in work when I get out.* Following my buddy's advice, I had purposely gained a decent chunk of weight. Shouldn't be a problem. I didn't exactly love the way I looked, but I assured myself *I'll be looking great by the time I'm out.* Plus a few days earlier I'd gone to the effort of deleting the first four years of my social media content. Not for any posts in particular. I just knew in a few weeks it would be some deeply depressed tabloid journalist intern's job to doomscroll through my public accounts and find a reason to write an article about something along the lines of I'm fighting with Rhonda Burchmore, lying about my age and probably having an affair with the guy who grooms my dog. Everything was in place for my new life as a C-grade reality star who used to do stand-up.

That morning, Kyran and I were walking to our local cafe just before 9 am when my phone rang. It was Kat. If the time the call came through wasn't enough of a clue, when I answered I could tell from the tone of her voice straight away that this wasn't going to be stupendous news. 'What's happening?' There was a lot of um-ing and ah-ing and wandering around the point but finally it became clear that I, a completely malaria- and rabies-immune comedian, had been bumped. Overnight she'd received an email and then this morning an early call letting her know that someone famous-er had become available so I was to be completely wiped from the cast. 'Next year, we promise!' they apparently said.

I was angry. So deeply grumpy. And just when I started getting over it the show went to air and I reached a whole new level of fury about who was actually in the show. 'I got bumped for these people?!' I shouted, catatonically drunk, yelling at the screen and to no one. 'Well this is a real who's who of who's that, isn't it? I don't even watch these fucking shows,' I'd blast while absolutely watching it. 'Why are people watching it? If I wanted to watch a pack of beautiful yet neurotic creatures fight it out for food only to be eliminated one by one, I'd hide a couple packs of aspirin in a loaf of bread and head down the duck pond.' I was beginning to sound like Bette Davis being interviewed during her later burning bridges years.

Luckily, to quote all delusional people when something annoying happens that they can't control: it was all for the best. During the time I would have been filming that show, I was asked to be an opening act for comedy legend Conan O'Brien when he toured Australia. That led to me appearing on his *Late Night* talk show, which got me an agent in the USA who helped me get a special on Netflix that RuPaul saw and then hired me onto *Drag Race Down Under*. Almost every year the show calls my agent and asks if we're interested. 'Next year, we promise.'

CULTURAL DIFFERENCES

The idea of consuming the food from other cultures has always been pretty exciting to me. You learn so much about a group of people by what they eat. I mean, the pure act of ingestion is one of the only things that truly links us all together as a species. That, and our all-in agreement that Margot Martindale continues to be a severely under-appreciated character actor who deserves more recognition. In my estimation, she has more than earnt the full June Squibb experience.

I am not a picky eater. It's one of the very few personality traits I have that doesn't haunt me to my core. In my early teen years I was a chubby little fella and I suppose the idea of limiting what I could eat seemed almost counterproductive. Why not try everything? If you're not willing to discover what you *don't* like, how can you ever be sure what you *do*? I'm not sure if that actually means anything, but it sounds like something someone might say in a book, so there you go. Thankfully I'm not particularly squeamish and can honestly say

I would try almost anything once. Unexpected textures, less desirable cuts of meat, that style of fine dining restaurant where it's one long table and you could find yourself – having paid a small fortune – sitting next to the toddler of an unhappy rich couple who spends the whole night smashing away at an iPad, in $800 dungarees and shouting about how she just wants plain spaghetti. I don't plan to wade into the debate of where children should and shouldn't go, and I'm most certainly not about making fine dining overly exclusionary, but I also don't think it's out of the question to perhaps simply offer a service at which you can cloak your child. Like a coat or a handbag.

I have this friend, well, friend is a strong word; he's really more of a person who's in my life and will continue to be until I do something about that. A sort of life barnacle. We're all someone's life barnacle. Each and every one of us has someone we are deeply interested in who clearly has no regard for our wellbeing. We nevertheless cling to their hulls in hopes of getting to where they're going. It's beautiful, really. My barnacle always has a lot of activewear on, has almost no sense of humour and is one of these people who claims to only eat food for fuel. What a tragic little lycra-clad steam train. He has zero curiosity in pushing his taste palate, even an inch. The very idea of properly dropping some cash on a meal out or ingredients to make one is, to him, needless and stupid. It's a point of view that's always been a real boner-shrinker for me. Even throughout the bouts in my life when a healthy diet and I didn't exactly see eye to eye, I've always felt food, in all its forms, should attract some level of reverence, of ceremony. Some ritual. It feels somehow disrespectful otherwise. Now, when I say ritual, I don't necessarily mean in a religious sense. In fact, the one and only time I ever took communion (a long story involving my primary school best friend's lesbian, born-again Christian mother taking us to a mega church one Sunday morning), it wasn't lost on me how underwhelming this whole wafer and wine business was. Even as a young child I was thinking, *I'm sorry, this is the body of your lord and saviour we're talking about here? So the metaphor you've come up with is a bone-dry cracker and some stale goon? Surely Jesus would be expecting something a little more considered? A bit more fun? He's always seemed like a foodie to me.* After all, one of the most famous images we have in the Western world is of him at a restaurant. Even though he knew he was going to die the next day, JC still thought he could figure it out while chowing down on a few share plates surrounded by his pals. Surely if the church was spending a little less time and energy hiding money and abusers, and a teensy bit more on the catering, maybe they wouldn't find themselves in such crashing decline. I'm just saying. Some nice bresaola and a few scattered shards of Manchego could really make mass pop off.

There are of course some gastronomical areas where I wouldn't tread, mostly for moral reasons. I try to be as sensitive as possible when talking about the dishes of other cultures. The likes of, say, shark fin soup might seem downright barbaric to you, but to someone raised on it, it's just a part of life. It has to be said, though, in some cases the word 'tradition' gets slung around so much it leads to overkill. Literally. My slightly batty high-school cooking teacher once went rogue from the curriculum and told the class about the now illegal French delicacy of ortolan bunting; a small, now endangered songbird that is vastly overfed then drowned/marinated in Armagnac. The feathers are plucked before it's roasted and then eaten completely whole in one bite. Customarily, diners are urged to wear napkins over their heads with the two-pronged benefit of being able to immerse themselves in the aroma of the recently murdered birdies, while also conveniently being able to hide from God. I still don't know how this came up, but our class sure was pretty quiet for the rest of the lesson.

I understand that some culturally significant dishes come from centuries of custom and convention, but this all sounds more like a dare to me. Some fourteenth-century French chef with a personality disorder because he wasn't allowed a budgie as a kid over-ordered on the brandy and got bored one afternoon. Thankfully, eating ortolan was officially banned by the French government in 1999, but you have to ask yourself, coming from the country that loves foie gras and eating whole calves' heads, how fucked-up does food have to be for even the French to be like, 'Oh la la, we better cool our jets on this one.'

Ortolan was not the most obscure culinary delight I learned about in school, however. I was publicly schooled. By that I mean I went to a public school, not that someone gave me a piece of their mind on the street. It was on the playground I first started to hear about the food practices of one demographic that fascinates me to this day: privately educated straight men. Now, don't get me wrong, I speak only with love. It's a captivating cohort with some very interesting practices. They're adorable! With their harsh fabrics and their violence. And war. That's them. We owe a lot to our, at times lost, hetero brethren. But their food? I've never been able to shake the memory of first hearing about what could only be described as their national dish. It was explained to me as almost a folktale about the peculiar goings on that were apparently happening at all-boys private boarding schools. It's a simple meal. Really more of a snack with only two ingredients. As with the ortolan, dishes of this ilk that are so significant to a community's sense of self are less about the parts and more about the way they are prepared. It is known by many different names, depending on the habitat of whichever privately educated straight man you're talking to, but is mostly commonly known as Soggy Biscuit. Many of you will know exactly what I'm talking about, but for some lucky few, I can only apologise for plucking you out of the warm embrace of ignorance. There's no long list of ingredients or tricky method to contend with. The ritual goes: if you were to have a whole stack of privately educated young males in a room (a sort of incubator of future leaders and law makers) and you were to chuck a packet of, oh, let's say, Saos in there, they'll eat most of them, sure. But when they find themselves down to the last one, something wildly unexpected is going to happen. A kind of race will occur. A terrible, terrible race. Yes, they're going to jerk off onto that cracker. All of them. Furiously they will work toward the ceremonious crescendo that arrives when the final participant, the 'loser' as it were, is urged to, and again I apologise, eat the biscuit.

As I say, you can learn a lot about a group by what they eat. Perhaps communion isn't too bad after all.

WILDLY BASIC VANILLA SLICE

This is a far more rewarding dessert snack and will lead to absolutely nil institutionalised bullying.

– SERVES: ONE–SIX –

– PREPARATION TIME: ABOUT 40 MINUTES PLUS THREE HOURS SETTING TIME –

– COOKING TIME: GETTING CLOSE TO AN HOUR, PLUS COOLING –

– INGREDIENTS –

2 sheets store-bought puff pastry, cut into 25 cm squares
500 ml milk
375 ml pouring cream
70 g butter, roughly chopped into adorable little buttery cubes
2 vanilla beans, split and seeds scraped (or 2 tbsp vanilla paste)
120 g caster sugar
40 g cornflour
6 egg yolks
icing sugar, to dust
absolutely zero cum

– METHOD –

- Start by not in any way ejaculating onto a single one of the ingredients, then preheat the oven to 200°C fan-forced (220°C conventional). Line two oven trays with baking paper and one 20 cm square cake tin so the paper extends above the rim for easy removal.

- Pop the pastry squares onto the oven trays and prick all over with a fork. It can be fun to write rude or aggressive messages to loved ones in morse code, if you have time. Don't cum on the pastry. Bake for 10–15 mins, until dark golden and puffed, swapping and turning the trays halfway through cooking so the squares cook evenly.

- Cool on wire racks, all the while making no attempt to put sperm on them. Now you can trim to neat 20 cm squares with a serrated knife and place one square in the base of the lined tin.

- Okay, let's make a little custard, shall we? Seems like an appropriate time. Pop the milk, cream, butter and vanilla in a saucepan and get it heading towards a simmer, but do not boil. Remember, zero semen in there. While that's happening, whisk the sugar, cornflour and yolks to form a smooth, golden paste. Gradually pour the milk mixture in, whisking continuously and doing your absolute darndest not to scramble the egg. Then return to the pan and whisk over a low heat until thick – 4–5 minutes. Remove from the heat, discard the vanilla beans (if using) and allow it to cool for a few minutes. Now pour over the pastry base in the tin. Press remaining pastry square on top and refrigerate until set (approx. 3 hours).

- Remove vanilla slice from tin and carefully cut into rectangles with a serrated knife. Dust with icing sugar and enjoy these beautiful golden giants having not once spilled seed on them.

HOW TO WRITE YOUR FIRST BOOK: PART IV

It's okay. It's fine. Fine. Fine. Fine. It's all fine. It's going to be fine.

STORY TIME

I'm often asked how I landed my job as judge on *RuPaul's Drag Race Down Under*. It's usually from journalists, sometimes randoms on the street and once, RuPaul herself. I always answer, 'Well, I went to drag legal school, was a drag paralegal, then a lawyer and eventually was appointed to the bench and now I'm a judge.' This has never, not once, elicited anything close to a laugh, but I persist. The truth is, I don't know. I have positively no idea how I was able to slither my way behind that desk, and I'm quite happy living in the dark about it. All I do know is I get paid to sit next to icons all day as I indulge in gorging myself on my lifelong most favourite art form: drag.

Somewhere around the age of eight or nine, I was sitting at the table of a dinner party being held at our neighbours' house. Their place was across the road and they were that type of waspy family who lived in the best house on the worst street within a less than ideal neighbourhood. A wealthy, uptight, privately educated and deeply religious family with strong connections to the local Catholic church, the entire household carried themselves in a way you could tell they thought – knew, even – they were better than us and the other heathens of the area. They weren't. These people were like the prized hogs on the farm. Bigger than us. Had better breeding. But at the end of the day, they were still just pigs living in shit with the rest of us. After the last bites were had of the severely under-spiced meal, the adults were nattering away and at some point all the kids present were asked what we wanted to be when we grew up. There were the usual adorable if predictable responses: doctor, teacher, vet. One of the boys said he wanted to work at his father's law firm, which I found creepy coming from someone barely able to cope with structured play. Then when it came to my turn, I exclaimed, with gusto, that I wanted to be a *drag queen.* A hush of silent moral panic heaved across the table until my parents nervously laughed and looked anywhere in the room but our hosts' eyes until, out of sheer discomfort, the lady of the house left for the kitchen and returned to serve up a lemon drizzle cake that was about as dry and tasteless as her marriage.

On the way home that night I wondered why my answer had brought the evening to such a standstill. I was confused. On my parents' request I'd tried to be on my best behaviour all evening. I'd thought I hadn't said anything that could be taken as uncouth. I'd pretended to enjoy the food. I didn't giggle as they said grace. I didn't even mention that their daughter, my age, had once asked to see my penis (a request I politely declined). What had I said that was so alarming? I wasn't joking – I really did want to be a drag queen. I still do.

I suppose some suburban god botherers could have been wondering how a preteen like me could even know what a drag queen was.

Well, like all decent, artsy parents worth their weight in therapy, my folks showed me the likes of *The Rocky Horror Picture Show* and *Priscilla, Queen of the Desert* perhaps a little early. The first time I saw the lavish colour and joyful movement happening on screen in *Priscilla*, I instantly knew this was some life-altering shit for someone in my position. Something I was going to need some more information about. As Mitzi, Bernadette and Felicia embodied the Sydney Opera House in a grim Alice Springs casino, I turned to my mother with wide eyes and asked, 'What are they doing?'

'Well,' she replied, 'They are doing drag. They are drag queens.' I was changed. Don't panic or call child services from your time machine. The Nicholson adults in the room were responsible and fast-forwarded through all the properly adult bits. Of course, because it was the '90s and on VHS, it does mean I still *kind* of saw them. Just a lot faster. During the abridged version of *The Rocky Horror Picture Show*, I didn't understand what Tim Curry was doing to Susan Sarandon atop that shadowy bed in the haunting countryside manor, but by the speed he was doing it in fast-forward, I knew he probably should book in a session or two of chiropractic realignment. Or at least get a neck massage.

There was a feeling that wasn't clear to me yet, but I was quickly drawn to these stories. Without connecting them to sex, whatever that was, the characters I saw were people living under some unknown pressure, yet were continuing on and squeezing as much out of their existence as humanly possible. Over the years it led me to leapfrog from *Priscilla* and *Rocky* to campier, more family-friendly titles like *The Birdcage* and over to *Victor/Victoria*. Then as I got older, to

Wigstock: The Movie, *Hedwig and the Angry Inch* and *Paris Is Burning* until finally, in my late teens, I laid my eyes on Divine for the first time and fell tits first into the opulent horrorscapes of John Waters' oeuvre. Sometimes we'd watch as a family and have huge conversations afterwards about what we saw. I learned about the AIDS crisis and why we have pride parades. I didn't know it at the time, but simply through ingesting all this bright, unrestrained enthusiasm for life on screen, I was constructing a little tapestry in my head. Without realising, I was mapping the history of a community I would soon, thank fuck, be a part of.

Decades later, I was sitting in an airport lounge, trying my hardest not to notice the Sky News programming they had blaring out the several TVs hung from practically every wall. The show was being hosted by fun conservative commentator Peta Credlin. A joy of a person who's really putting the word 'party' into 'ex-advisor to the Liberal Party'. She was participating in a panel discussion about some protests being held to stop an event called Drag Story Time from happening at a library. *What is Drag Story Time?* I imagine hearing you ask. Well, for one, it's the working title of my unauthorised biography about the career of Barry Humphries, but it's also a series of gatherings that take place in many countries around the world that give drag performers in all their colourful finery an opportunity to volunteer their time to read books to children in libraries. Seems innocent enough, right? Well, as it turns out, over the past little while they've been facing a growing amount of backlash from the right and have inspired some violent objections. Sadly, there's oodles of footage online. You can see infuriated demonstrators picketing public libraries across the globe, where demonstrators scream, 'STAY AWAY FROM THE KIDS!' Some rogue demonstrators have sent threats of violence and even death to event organisers and performers. Yeah, let's get the kids around *that* energy. That seems safe.

I'd started to watch the TV just as Peta sledged, 'You know, my issue isn't about drag queens, or trans people, porno stars, even hetero story book readers there in skimpy bathers. Any of those is inappropriate.' If you caught it, she's comparing drag queens and trans people to porn actors. Hey, it could be worse, she could have lumped them in with *Sky News* presenters! At least the stories in porn are more believable. As the conversation trudged on, the panel kept coming back to this point about 'protecting the children'. 'Can't we just let kids be kids?' Credlin cried. 'And have people with their clothes on who are just focused on reading the book, rather than all of this provocative theatre?' Hey Peta, I agree with you. Can't we let kids be kids and not have them used as political footballs to be bashed around anytime you get confused by a gender-neutral bathroom? Why can't you just comment on the real news? Hmm? Rather than create all this provocative and hurtful theatre?

When I was younger, something that always stuck out to me in the queer films I was gobbling up was that the villains of the stories were always tense, conservative types who at the very whiff of a lifestyle they didn't completely understand, launched straight into fear and catastrophe. Even back then I vaguely sensed a feeling they were always trying to protect the world from so-called degusting reprobates who had dared to live with a modicum of fun and authenticity. As I grew, I discovered these self-appointed morality police were in fact very real and actually quite noisy. I feel sorry for them. Truly. It must be so exhausting to be so scared all the time. Scared of analysing yourself. Scared to question. Scared of rattling the status quo. Scared of stretching your idea of what happiness is. Thank living fuck my parents made the wild choice to screen *Priscilla* and *The Rocky Horror*, particularly with their own hasty fast-forwarded edits. I am so, so lucky to have the family I have. Both biological and chosen. I'm not even sure if they knew they were doing it, but when my blindingly straight parents showed me – their odd, camp little kid – the optimistic, shiny more wondrous elements of the queer world without any connection to sex or the never-ending geyser of outright tragedy our community has experienced, I was able to take a tiny peek into what it can feel like to live genuinely. I could see what a dreamy group the queers are. Imagine not wanting your child to live their life under the refrain of 'Don't Dream it, Be It'? I grew up knowing there is just nothing inherently sexual about drag. If you think there is, you maybe need to talk to someone about your carnal feelings towards hip pads and glitter eye shadow. Drag is about joy and love and dare I sound so naive, hope. Every huge moment for queer people, every leap forward and setback we've achieved, there, at the barricades, are the drag queens and kings, throwing the first bricks, sometimes literally. They are the frontline personification of a community reaching for equality. Whereas the other people, the bossy brigade, are worried about queens indoctrinating and sexualising children. I don't know, between the Dalai Lama asking a young boy to suck his tongue and the Catholic Church's whole, you know, *vibe*, I'm not sure drag queens are the men in dresses we should be keeping kids away from.

RHYS NÍCHOLSON

A WILDLY BASIC LEMON DRIZZLE TEA CAKE FOR SAD STRAIGHT PEOPLE

– SERVES: SIX–EIGHT SAD HETEROSEXUALS –

– PREPARATION TIME: ABOUT TWENTY MINUTES –

– COOKING TIME: AN HOUR-ISH –

– INGREDIENTS –

Cake

1¾ cups plain flour

1½ tsp baking powder

¼ tsp salt

110 g unsalted butter, softened

1 cup granulated sugar

2 large eggs

zest 2 lemons

1 tsp vanilla extract

½ cup whole milk

Lemon drizzle

juice 2 lemons

¼ cup granulated sugar

Glaze

1 cup icing sugar
2 tbsp lemon juice

– METHOD –

- Before you preheat your oven to 195°C and grease and line a 22 × 12 cm loaf tin with baking paper, hop on Facebook and share a very pixelated meme about the perceived negative effects a socially marginalised group is bringing to the world.
- In a medium bowl, stir together the flour, baking powder and salt. Set aside.
- In a large bowl, use a stand or hand mixer to cream together the softened butter and sugar until light and fluffy.
- Add the eggs one at a time, mixing well after each addition. Stir in the lemon zest and vanilla extract.
- Gradually add the dry ingredients to the butter mixture, alternating with the milk. Begin and end with the dry ingredients, mixing until just combined. Be careful not to overmix.
- Pour the batter into the prepared loaf tin and smooth the top with a spatula.

- Bake for 45–50 minutes, or until a skewer inserted into the centre of the cake comes out clean.

- While the cake is baking, prepare the lemon drizzle by heating the lemon juice and caster sugar in a small saucepan over low heat until the sugar has dissolved. Remove from the heat and leave to cool.

- When the cake is done, remove from the oven and place the tin on a wire rack. While the cake is still warm, poke several holes on the top with a skewer. Pour the lemon drizzle over the cake, allowing it to soak into the holes and spread across the top.

- Let the cake cool completely in the tin before removing it.

- In a small bowl, whisk together the icing sugar and lemon juice to make the glaze. Drizzle the glaze over the cooled cake.

- Allow the glaze to set before slicing and serving.

SMALLEST TALK

It can be hard to know where you fit in. I love to play video games. Astonishingly violent ones. The type where you really smash the shit out of things and cause catastrophic havoc to innocent pixels. I find it very relaxing. But, even though I enjoy playing video games, I will always be nervous to call myself a 'gamer' in polite conversation. Partly because when you come out to someone with no knowledge of that world, their minds automatically spring to some clichéd idea of what that actually means. They think of incels and teenagers alike wearing headsets, hunched over expensive, customised tech accessories as they battle it out with each other online under socially reductive screen names. It's a nasty stereotype. On the other side of the controller, though, I am careful how I refer to myself in the company of actual serious computing athletes; they would probably find how I play rudimentary and offensive to their kind. And look, I just don't want to anger such a huge pack of dangerous virgins.

Not too long ago, Kyran and I went to a dinner at a restaurant that was one of those situations where you find yourself among a hodgepodge of invitees. Our host works in a very vague, wide-ranging part of the creative arts with an ever-changing job title that no one will admit they don't understand, so the guestlist was a sort of potpourri of personalities, with each element more overwhelming than the last. On arrival, the two of us were sat next to each other at the end of a long table. A few moments after we'd settled in, my beloved made the treacherous decision to start a conversation with a close friend of his sitting diagonally opposite. The side I wasn't sat at. I had no way in. He had essentially thrown me into a conversational penal colony, so I had no choice but to look over to the stranger across from me. I'm not completely averse to meeting new people, but these types of evenings can sometimes feel more like a social experiment than an enjoyable night out. You have to put on a little play for new people. Give them a sizzling highlights reel of your life and opinions in the hopes they want to watch the whole series. You know – friendship.

I really don't need any new friends. I'm tired. So what's the point of this whole charade? This isn't gloating. I'm not exactly drowning is companionship, I'm just barely holding on to the ones I have now. I'm a bad buddy. I'm terrible at replying to texts, emails, phone calls, I'm not certain of any of the names of my friends' children and under the right circumstances, the cancellation of plans will get me physically aroused. At this point I'm a couple of missed haircuts and a few mason jars of urine away from going full Howard Hughes.

Back in the restaurant, my neighbour and I introduced ourselves and exchanged some pleasantries and then, out of nowhere, he asked if I thought I was a cat or a dog person. I internally bristled. *Fuck, we are barely a few minutes into this affair but have already somehow completely run out of things to say to one another?* Nevertheless, I obliged. I explained I have a dog. A female, purebred, Welsh springer spaniel named Sir Anthony Hopkins, who through a series of self-inflicted health issues over the years has brought us to the brink of financial ruin no less than three times. I tried to be funny and charming to carry the question.

'She has a fucking birth certificate!' I remember saying. 'We paid extra for a nice but clearly bonkers lady who lives in the country with far too many dogs in her house, to register her. I don't know with whom, but now I know for certain that our pet is alive. At gunpoint I couldn't tell you where my birth certificate is, but I could fetch you hers in a matter of seconds. How many points of ID does she need? Will we be applying for her boating licence come summer?'

He kind of smiled and then asked if we ever want kids. Ooft, another non sequitur? As we kept on going and I explained my usual, prepared, conversational material about childrearing, it became clearer that no, these questions weren't, as I had suspected, a desperate attempt to resuscitate a deceased conversation. He's just one of those 'big questions' kinds of people. You know the ones. Cheery sorts with huge smiles and dead eyes. They've confused the category of questions an email password protection bot might use to identify you with actual conversation. They end up treating a friendly interaction more as a survey. In my opinion, these questions aren't too dissimilar to any and all queries about your zodiac sign or food allergies; a sly way for a person with too much time on their hands and not enough iron in their diet to think they're getting a read on you. When you're asked these big swings, it always feels as if no matter what your answer is, your charmless interlocutor is making some massive assumptions. Your whole vibe is being assessed, calibrated and filed away for some unknown future use. Before we'd even finished our starters, I had a little label pinned on me because of the big reveal that I'm a 'dog person'.

This isn't how I operate. The huge queries don't do anything for me because most people already have their points of view thought through on those topics. You're not getting to the nut of someone. You're getting readymade talking points. There's nothing new there. For me, the real key to someone is small talk. The smallest of talk, barely visible to the naked eye. Near minuscule.

I couldn't care less if you're a feline or canine type. I see very little insight coming from knowing that. As long as we can all agree that people who have a lot of reptiles in their homes are to be avoided at all costs, we'll get on just fine. One gecko? Okay, sure. It's not great but it can be looked over as a quirk you can slowly wring out of someone if you're going to invest in this friendship. However, as soon as it's veering into multiple iguana territory, I think their internet activity should be monitored because, I'm sorry, there is absolutely something going on in that house.

As our mains and a few simple, green side salads were placed on the table, I was trying and failing to bring Kyran into the fold to save me. This is when my new best friend asked the other one that gets me every time.

'What's your favourite film?'

Ergh. Is there a question more saturated – dripping, almost – in judgement? It always comes at a moment when you know for a fact the person asking isn't actually listening. They are just waiting for you to finish whatever tosh a nincompoop like you might be blathering on about so he (it's almost always a he) can corner you with their forty-minute discourse on what makes for quality cinema. 'I think it's the scenes Sophia Coppola *doesn't* film that make her work really interesting. Oh, and have you heard they're doing a retrospective of David Lynch's early work? It's just got a limited run down an alley in Brooklyn, being projected solely onto Isabella Rossellini's lower back.' If you listen closely you can hear orifices of all kinds begin to snap shut around the room when 'Oh, I'm really only into subtitled movies' is uttered. That is a real thing a real person said to me a number of years ago. Unless you are hard of hearing, that makes absolutely no sense. Hey, don't get me wrong, I truly do love international cinema as much as the next pseudo intellectual in a pair of wide-legged pleated pants, but they're not called readies. Buy a book if you're that keen to spend your leisure time immersed in words. It's a line of enquiry that was acceptable around a hundred years ago I reckon, when we, the cinema-adoring public, only had a handful of films to choose from. My kingdom to be a film critic in the 1800s! 'I liked the loop of the running horse and that one where the moon has a face, but I must admit, the train coming out of the tunnel frightened me and I had to leave the salon lecture screaming with terror. Three stars out of five.'

Usually, whenever I'm asked about my particular tastes in film, I'll have the same reaction as almost everyone else: I attempt a vague, nonchalant reach for the stars. A kind of catch-all statement to give no specific answer at all. 'Well, *The Departed* is almost perfect. Anything by Scorsese, of course. Soderbergh, Taika, Jane Campion. I just like a great narrative, really. Characters! Characters are good in a movie.

I think I like it most when the characters and story are good. It's fantastic when there are good parts in a movie with good characters and plot.' That's what I usually do. But as we served ourselves salad, I decided to try some big talk. See how it felt.

'My favourite movie is *The First Wives Club*, actually,' I told him. He looked confused. 'But speaking of film,' I continued, 'As I get older the porn that I look at is changing. Have you noticed that?'

'Oh um, I, ah.'

'Years ago in my teens and early twenties, I'd basically look at anything. It all worked. Very shiny American stuff. These days my search terms have changed. Firstly, amateur porn. I only look at amateur stuff. I need to believe they are a real couple. I need to believe they are in love. I like it if they are . . . how can I say this? I like it if they feel attainable. I'd like to feel like I could get in there and not be told to leave. It helps if they're clearly renting. I'm not sure why that is. Last year I was actually working on a TV show in Canada and one of my co-stars urged me to get one of those VR headsets so we could play video games on set in-between filming. Well, as I'm sure you can imagine, I get this contraption home and my curiosity gets the better of me. I decided to look up some porn. See what it's like. It was wild. Suddenly I'm *in* the video. There's this guy there doing all sorts of stuff to me. But I couldn't move past the fact it wasn't me! I'd look down and there was this honking big porno actor's junk down there. Took me right out of it. Also, how are they filming it? Is there some weird camera on the guy's head? Lovely house though. I had a look around and there was some stunning mid-century pieces around the room. To be honest, I would have preferred a tour of the house.'

'Oh, ah, interesting,' he eked out. 'I'm just going to go to the bathroom.'

When he returned, he found a reason to talk to the woman next to him and we didn't speak again all night. Some people just don't know good conversation.

A WILDLY BASIC, GROWN-UP RESTAURANTY GREEN SIDE SALAD

I had always wondered why the simplest of simple-looking green salads at a restaurant were always so delicious. What are they doing back there? It turns out there's this thing called salt and these other things called herbs.

If you're a foody type of person, this is not a recipe. It's an insult. Please don't bother reading the rest of this section because you'll wonder why it's in here and, you know what? Go fuck yourself. Simply realising I could just add some herbs and a little sea salt to a few leaves and mixing together something acidic with olive oil without hyperbole changed the way I eat during the week. There are a bazillion people out there just living their lives either not having salad at all or worse, squeezing some grim leaves out of a sealed bag of premixed four leaf combo, drenching it in balsamic and going on their merry way. There's a better, far fibrous life out there. This ain't no Ottolenghi test kitchen experience. It's fundamental as fuck and it's the gateway drug to eating more greens. Once you open this door you can start changing up the textures with sliced of fennel, radishes, blah blah blah.

Speaking as someone with some fun and completely undiagnosed gut health situations going on, I love a nice, big, green side salad with anything. It's nature's Metamucil. Also speaking as a busy mum, I tend to make a massive batch of the greens at the start of the week and keep it in an airtight container in the fridge so I can scoop out a couple handfuls as an accompaniment to any weeknight meals. It's so basic it almost feels offensive to call it a recipe, but I just really, really like it. The (legal) herbs we have growing on our balcony are mainly for this salad. Parsley, dill and tarragon are pretty easy to keep alive, and you feel way less like a dick buying punnets of them at the supermarket for $5 only to forget about them and then buying some more three days later.

It works with pretty much any dressing, but something like a basic vinaigrette with either lemon or shallots will cut through any meaty boy or rich main you have going on. There are a couple options down here.

– SERVES: FOUR –

– PREPARATION TIME: TWENTY MINUTES –

– INGREDIENTS –

Greens

1 head butter lettuce, ripped apart and torn up a bit

2 heaped cups rocket

4 radishes, super thinly sliced

1 cup parsley leaves and soft stems, roughly chopped
½ cup dill, torn up
⅓ cup tarragon leaves (French or regular)
a healthy little mound of flaky sea salt

- For the salad itself, just whack it all into a big bowl and toss. Like, for Christ's sake. Well, I mean everything except the salt. Add that after you've dressed it so the flakes are all through and stick to the glossy leaves.

Easy shallot vinaigrette

1 medium French shallot, peeled and chopped into itty bitty bits (essentially minced)
2 tbsp white wine vinegar
1 tsp Dijon mustard
about a pinch of sugar
¼ cup decent olive oil
salt and pepper, to taste

- Put the shallot into a small mixing bowl and add the vinegar. Allow to sit for 10–15 minutes.

- Add the mustard and sugar and then while whisking pretty vigorously gradually pour in the oil until it's emulsified. Season to taste, and then put however much dressing feels right for you over the salad. There's quite a bit going on so you should only need enough to get the salad glossy, not wet.

Easy lemon vinaigrette

zest ½ lemon

2 tbsp lemon juice

1 tsp Dijon mustard

1 tsp honey or maple syrup

¼ cup decent olive oil

salt and pepper, to taste

- Pop the lemon zest, juice, Dijon and honey into a medium bowl and whisk vigorously while gradually pouring in the oil until it's combined. Season to taste. A bunch of pepper is nice.

SHIPWRECKED

'So you can't say "cunt",' the voice down the line says.

'Alright,' I reply.

'Or make any jokes about the ship sinking.'

'Oh, of course.'

'It's always called a ship. Never call it a boat. And don't tease the captain. That's a big one.'

I was on a call to a to live comedy producer having the rules explained to me for an upcoming run of gigs. In a few days time I would be spending a long weekend performing on a cruise ship as it did doughnuts in international waters off the coast of Sydney.

'Oh, and the main one,' she said, suddenly sounding quite serious. 'Under no circumstances are you to have any sex, of any kind, with any of the passengers.' I often multitask by doing some washing in my apartment building's shared laundry while taking work calls. 'Yes, but can I have sex with the captain?' I queried as I hit start on a load of whites and turned around. Standing in the doorway was the downstairs neighbour I don't know very well. She was holding a basket of delicates and looked a little startled by what she'd just heard. Pointing at my phone I mouthed, 'Sorry, work,' then squeezed past her.

Cruise ships don't exactly have the best reputation among the wider comedian population. Much like a boat itself, it's generally thought a comic's value starts to really depreciate as soon as they hit the open water. I'd spent years as an open mic-er in comedy club backstages as the older, wearier performers discussed the ship comics as if they were this sort of radicalised splinter group of our community. 'She was great,' they would lament. 'Then she got stuck on the ships. Her whole act is for cruises now.' The word 'stuck' was thrown around a lot. As if saying yes to this line of work was in some way against their free will and under dubious circumstances. Like they had followed some siren's call to certain, watery doom. Now their grief-stricken mothers lit candles in windows and prayed hopelessly for the safe return of these sons and daughters lost tragically at sea. But, to be fair, it was also unanimously suspected that the buffet on board is quite good.

The night before I left I was packing and noodling around on some online forums looking for any hacks or clever suggestions of what to bring on a cruise. I truly had no idea. There's a lot of chat about sea sickness tablets and extra sunscreen. One lady suggested mace. But then a clickbait article sidetracked me. It claimed studies are showing a trend in the popularity of cruising with retired senior citizens. Apparently due to the ever-escalating costs of living, mixed in with the beginning of much more affordable cruising holidays, more and more pensioners these days are rejecting rest homes as a retirement option and instead spending their final days on the ships.

I mean, I get it. Why resign yourself to drab nursing homes with mushy food and systemic elder abuse when you could be island hopping in a light linen pantsuit with a balcony stateroom and exchanging small talk over cocktails on the poop deck with handsome, exotic-looking men who are paid to flirt with you? Essentially what this article was saying was: aged care is so broken in this country that we've forced a bunch of old people into going out to sea to die. A kind of fun, longform Viking funeral. I placed a third bottle of sunscreen into my half-packed bag and wondered if in some way I was doing the same thing.

When you're in your early twenties you sure have a lot of big opinions about things you won't do. Especially if you work in any kind of creative field. No one has more integrity and less talent than a twenty-year-old with artistic aspirations. When I was a little baby comedian I don't remember performing that much, but I do remember talking a lot about performing. Myself and the other open mic-ers would gather together in venue smoking areas and wax lyrical about the types of shows we would do and more importantly the types of shows that just wouldn't get us. My art wasn't for everyone. That was clear. And by 'art' I mean a four-minute story where I explain in great detail the single day in my recent teenage years when I tried to masturbate ten times (a true and in retrospect quite harrowing story). I recall some of the work I turned down back then and think to myself, *My god, what was I on?* Then I remember it was mostly MDMA and, occasionally, speed. So yeah, that makes sense now. But then as you drift slowly into your late twenties and then plummet turbulently into your early thirties, perspectives start to shift. You find yourself being a little less, shall we say, picky. Some of these new views creep in slowly as if they are trying not to wake you, and some snap in like an occy strap to the face. At twenty-one I have a distinct memory of loudly and very drunkenly telling my housemate that I will never get married, will live alone forever and most of all I will never, ever be one of those hacks doing shitty corporate gigs and depressing cruise ships. Just under a decade later and after kissing my fiancé goodbye and leaving our little house, I stood in line, passport in hand, to enter the brave new world of Cruiseland. At this pace of change, by my calculations I expect to be a straight, twice-divorced, conservative Queensland senator by my mid-forties.

At a small cafe in a weird part of town near the frankly enormous docked ship, all the acts met up before we boarded. It was the style of cafe that only pops up in country towns or near airports and where the coffee comes in two sizes. A cup or a mug. And no matter what you choose it's pretty clear the staff are furious you're even there. I ordered a frankly enormous vanilla slice and sat down to join the other performers. Around the vinyl gingham tablecloth sat a musical comedian in his late fifties, a worryingly old clowning duo, a magician who was so overly fake-tanned it was hard to tell if he was a good forty-five or a bad thirty, our producer and me. It was an eclectic bunch. We looked like we had gathered together to do one last big heist. As the others nattered away and gossiped about their last cruise and which entertainment director was fucking which medical officer, my gut began to tie itself into a knot. Looking around the rest of the coffee shop I realised I was soaking in the demographic. These were the passengers. This was the audience. With their loud synthetic shirts, mini fedoras, walking frames and neck braces. None of it intended with a hint of irony. These weren't the inner city, woke, elitist douchebags I was used to performing for. This was 'Real Australia'. All of a sudden I felt well and truly out of my depth. The anxiety wasn't allayed when our producer announced the Captain had mentioned to expect some pretty rough seas for this trip.

'There's a huge fucking storm just offshore we'll have to get through,' she dropped far, far too casually. 'We'll be fine, but they might have to cancel the acrobats tonight.'

We gathered our things and headed towards the boarding area. Inside a huge barn-like building I was genuinely astonished by the sheer number of people. Rows and rows of what I would later find out call themselves 'Cruiselings'. I couldn't see a single male who didn't have a pair of sunglasses sitting on the back of his neck. As an older man walked by, he clocked me and cheerfully announced to my face, 'Your hair's different!' It definitely felt like he was actually saying, 'I don't understand your generation and I think they are a waste!' but I could be projecting.

As our group progressed through the check-in hall, a strapping man in all white who is best described as being a drawing of an American, greeted us by saying, 'Almost there, guys. Soon you'll be in Cruiseland.' I wanted to tell him Cruiseland sounded like an all-nude, gay theme park and resort where the hotel rooms don't have doors, but I figured I should get onto the ship before I make any new friends. The others glided through the several check-in levels making it look easy as I fumbled and stop-started my way forwards. Elderly passengers overtook me while I struggled to find the right paperwork and get into the correct line. Trying to focus myself, I was struck with the thought, *Whoever believed it was a good idea to put fucking acrobats on a ship? And what would happen if they didn't cancel them?* I imagined a twenty-something, fresh out of circus school, desperate to prove to his rural family that this dream was going to be profitable. He's up on one of those silk cloths dangling from the ceiling as ten-metre-high waves bash against the hull. The ship rocking and swaying from side to side. What would be going through his head as he swayed and yo-yoed uncontrollably? The screams muffled by the audience's loud hooting and hollering because they have no idea this was in fact not at all part of the show. I thought about him, and I felt a little bit better. At least all I was being paid to do was stand in front of a microphone and say funny shit, right?

After what felt like an eternity, I found myself on the gangway, shuffling towards the final entry point of the boat. Sorry, ship. I was surrounded by so many pensioners I could be forgiven for thinking we were boarding the vessel to cross the River Styx. I wondered if the boatman to the afterlife is still only taking coins or would he ever go cashless. I bet he must be getting an earful from all the Karens who only brought their pennies. I made it to the front of the line, my boarding card was scanned and I was, at last, welcomed into Cruiseland.

The first thing that hits you about Cruiseland is the smell. Clean. It smells very, very clean. Crime scene clean. Long before COVID was even a twinkle in a bat's eye, the most hand sanitiser dispensers I have ever seen were at sea. The second thing I noticed was that everything, and I mean everything, is glued down: sculptures, paintings, pot plants, each and every pebble around the plant. There are cameras everywhere. Everyone's in white. It's all so precise. Two women walked past me, one with a bright, glittering lanyard around her red neck. Clearly a seasoned Cruiseling, she was walking with purpose and talking at her companion. As they went by I heard her say, 'Oh we love it on here. Best bit is kids just disappear and we know they're safe, you know?' I mean absolutely. What could go wrong with that point of view? Where could a kid possibly go on the deck of a boat?

When I arrived at my room, it was exactly what you'd expect. Everything was smooth, clean and glassy but it all felt a little outdated. Peering through the small, round porthole window on the wall I spied my view – a lifeboat. Then when I opened the small closet, the first thing I saw was a life jacket. How lovely to be in a space that wherever I looked I could be reminded straight away of the worst-case scenario. This theme continued with a muster station check-in at which large groups of people were told by staff what to do in an emergency. I half-listened in the same way I do with airline safety announcements. It's with the understanding that if something happens, there's no hope of me surviving so why take up any more room in my tired brain with some sinking ship malarky about lights, whistles and big silver doors that apparently close and can't be opened again? As the ship set off, everyone on the top deck cheered as if we were headed to some new world and not international waters so they could open the casino.

I met up with the rest of the performers and our producer and we ate and had a drink. I didn't have a show that night so I was free to enjoy a few drinks and soak up the atmosphere. It was immediately clear that mid-afternoon is a strange time in Cruiseland. The mood is almost oppressive. I suppose it's because the passenger's lunchtime cocktails have set in hard and they are on the precipice of crashing before their naps at four thirty. There is an almost zombie-like ambience to the entire vessel.

I found myself hours later with our producer in the smoking area with one of the onboard medical officers. As the producer struck up a conversation with a passenger, I took the opportunity to lightly interrogate this crewmember. She was about my age, with a London accent. She was off-duty and like me had had a few dry white wines. Something had been on my mind for weeks. 'Hey, as the medical person, maybe you can tell me something.'

'Mmmhhhmmm?' Her eyes narrowed as she took a drag of her cigarette.

'I read this thing that said elderly people have started living out here on the boats—'

'It's a ship.'

'Yes the ships. So, like . . . If they're living out here, do they ever die out here?'

She squished out her durry then began rummaging through the purse as she matter-of-factly replied, 'Of course they do, babes.'

'Right. So what do you do with them?'

'Well,' she looked up. 'Pop 'em in the morgue.'

'There's a morgue?'

'Of course there's a bloody morgue.' She lit another cigarette and leant in close to me. 'I tell you something funny, though. Sometimes they cruise around out here for weeks. And the slightly older ships, like this one, they only have little, teeny tiny morgues. Limited space, you understand?'

I did not understand.

'Well, let's just say if ever you're on the top deck and they start handing out free ice cream . . .'

Jesus Christ. That night I lay in bed, drunk and absolutely haunted by the idea. Maybe she was just bullshitting me? Was this some sort of hazing? I mean, how? How are they keeping them in here? Are they on a bed? Is it a large cool room you might see at the back of a bottle shop? Is it more of a top-loader style? Are they rolling over poor, deceased eighty-eight-year-old Marlene to get to a bag of frozen crinkle cut chips?

The following days seemed pretty uneventful, really. There was a gong show where passengers performed and the comics gave feedback, a question-and-answer format where most of the questions were about political correctness going mad and one enquiry where the woman clearly thought I was Joel Creasey, then it was a few hours away from my solo late show and the following morning we'd be back home. At lunch our producer told us she'd been chatting with one of the higher-ups and after days of dodging the storm, in order to get home for tomorrow morning we'd have to go straight through it. 'We'll start heading inland about 10 pm they reckon. It could get pretty fucking rocky.'

'What time's my show tonight?'

She winced slightly. 'Ten thirty.'

Heading towards the showroom that is inexplicably at the very, very front of the ship, I saw that all the outdoor decks were closed.

On my way I was whacked by a series of tableaux that gave me the general vibe of the ship's mood. I saw the lanyard women from the first day restraining one of her children as he scream cried and at the top of a flight of stairs a cleaner wearing gloves and a plastic apron was creating a barrier of caution signs and what looked like biohazard tape around a huge puddle of sick. 'Good evening, sir,' she said.

Is it?

Backstage, I sat quietly with the producer waiting to go on. The ship was see-sawing from side to side and sometimes back to front. We could hear huge waves slapping at the side of the ship as if it had refused to remove the name of Will Smith's wife from its mouth. She put her hand on my shoulder and said I was booked to do forty minutes but none would be looking at the clock, so if I needed to get off after thirty-five, that was totally fine.

The next morning the sun beamed in through my porthole, bouncing off the unused lifeboat. The exit from the shitstorm was far more straightforward than the entry.

I got home and squeezed my fiancé. After dinner I slumped on the couch, weary from my adventures in the far-off kingdom of Cruiseland.

'Oh!' exclaimed Kyran. 'I got us a little treat.' He left for the kitchen and returned moments later proudly holding two almond mini Magnums. 'Ice cream?'

'Oh, um. No thank you.'

HOMETOWN GORY

It can be so nice to still have moments of discovery with your partner, even after years of blissful togetherness. A few Christmases ago we were in my hometown, Newcastle, when my uncle took my sister, Ceara, her partner Kensie, Kyran and I out on his new boat for a spot of fishing. Firstly, Kyran was shocked at the very notion I would be interested in an activity of this nature. I understand why, I suppose. The whole time we've been together, the most he's ever seen me near water is on Sundays, when I sit in the bath for about four hours, drinking gin sodas and watching forgotten, early 2000s police procedurals such as *Cold Case* (a real thing I do and I just can't recommend it enough). We headed out into the ocean and I was tickled pink at how quickly I caught a flathead. And then another. Then a bream. This was all well and good but the true shock for Kyran came when we arrived back ashore and as the boat was being hosed off, my uncle got to work at descaling and gutting the fish. Something in me asked if I could help and Kyran looked on, eyes wide with astonishment as my sense memories of this task from decades before came flooding back and I began ripping the wet innards of our fallen fish pals out with gusto and throwing them to the seagulls and pelicans who waited nearby. It was quiet for a bit until Kyran exclaimed, 'Your Newcastle is showing.'

As long as I've been alive, Newcastle has been known around the country for its beautiful beaches, remarkable surfing and fishing, our love of rugby league football and, in the early to mid-2000s, for its astonishingly high production of methamphetamines. There is an undeniable feeling of hostility bubbling up through the streets of Newie – the whole area, in fact. In the neighbouring township of Branxton there is a sign as you enter that reads: 'Welcome to Branxton. We have two cemeteries and no hospital. Drive carefully.' Is that a threat, Braxton?

We aren't quite right in Newcastle, and I'm proud of that. I've always thought a hometown is a macro version of your family. You think it's all normal and fine and then you bring someone home for Christmas and at the stroke of midnight, as your boomer relative is doing a handstand and smacking his feet together as everyone else loudly chants, 'Stand on your head and click you heels together! Stand on your head! Stand on your head!' you catch eyes with your date and realise everyone in your bloodline is fucking unhinged.

I was in my twenties before I realised not everyone grew up with Maurie the Mole as a part of their lives. Who is Maurie the Mole? Great question. You see, as a proud coal mining town since the 1800s, Newcastle is absolutely riddled with abandoned mine shafts. It's Swiss cheese down there. And wouldn't you know it, by the 1990s kids were fallin' down those damn mine shafts at an alarming rate. I suppose at some point the locals started asking the council questions like, 'Whaddya gonna do about all these kids in these holes?' and 'Are you going to fill in these holes?' and 'Has anyone seen my kids? They said they were going to go play around the mines.' So the council, in all their wisdom, thought about it and lo and behold, Maurie the Mole was born. Maurie was a terrifying seven-foot-tall cartoon mole wearing head to toe mining gear while holding a pickaxe who appeared on local TV ads to warn us about the dangers of open cut mines. You'd see a plush costumed version of Maurie at football games, the Newcastle Show and various other public events always spouting his famous catchphrase, 'If you see a hole, don't think you're a mole. Walk in the opposite direction and report your detection.' Not since Nike's 'Do it' has such a catchy slogan captured the hearts and minds of the youth.

What always got me about this jolly rodent was that he was always smiling. There he was in all his workwear grinning from beady eye to beady eye. I have a distinct memory of thinking as a kid, *Look at how happy this miner is! I gotta get myself down these mines.* Surely a more useful character could have been something along the lines of Heather the Head-injured Hippo with her famous phrase, 'I can't remember whole sections of last year.' But will the council reply to my numerous emails about this? No.

With Newcastle being a beach-y town, we grew up eating a lot of seafood in my extended family. As soon as your infant fine motor skills would allow, you were indoctrinated and put to work on

Christmas Day to help shell prawns, mix thousand island dressing and flour different species of cephalopods for frying. I've never been very good at making those light, bright, fresh-tasting ocean delights my uncle and aunts prepare. I don't have their gift of the barbecue arts. I much prefer making something more continental and that relies on butter.

I started this deeply basic version of the French classic, sole meunière, a few years ago after watching *Julie and Julia* while quite drunk and emotional on tour. I googled what in the world was that incredible-looking fish dish Meryl and Stanley Tucci eat in the scene where she decides to become a cook. Turns out it's a wildly simple traditional French meal that's a piece of white fish cooked fast in oil or clarified butter if you can be bothered, then decorated with some browned butter, lemon and herbs. It's luxurious, rich but also somehow delicate. Like Emily Blunt.

I've made it with a full flounder plenty of times and it's an almost mirror image process, but if you're looking to be a little less theatrical and perhaps cooking for someone who isn't mad about eating something as it makes eye contact with you, just get some nice big fillets.

Serve whatever you want as the side pieces but I like sticking to theme with some mash that is so buttery the potato starts to feel like just a middleman and you could have probably just eaten some cubes of butter, and green beans with, you guessed it, butter.

WILDLY BASIC FLAT FISH MEUNIÈRE WITH PARIS MASH AND GREEN BEANS FOR TWO (IT'S MOSTLY JUST BUTTER)

– SERVES: TWO –

– PREPARATION TIME: ABOUT HALF AN HOUR –

– COOKING TIME: ALL UP ABOUT AN HOUR –

– INGREDIENTS –

The beans

400 g green beans, trimmed

¼ cup red onion, chopped finely

3 tbsp unsalted butter

2 tbsp parsley, chopped finely

1 tbsp fresh thyme leaves

2 tbsp tarragon, chopped finely

salt and pepper

1 lemon, cut into wedges

The mash

500 g creamy potatoes (Dutch cream, desiree), cut into 2.5 cm cubes

100 g unsalted butter, cold and cubed

¼–½ cup warmed milk

salt and pepper

The fish

½ cup plain flour

2 decent-sized flat fish fillets

salt and pepper

around 1 cup plain flour

4 tbsp clarified butter (see below for a how to)

4 tbsp salted butter

2 tbsp capers, roughly chopped

juice 1 lemon

2 heaped tbsp chopped continental parsley

– METHOD –

The beans

- Start by bringing a big ol' pot of salted water to a rolling boil then make yourself a separate big ol' bowl of ice water. Blanch the beans in the boiling water for 2–2½ minutes. They should be *bright* green. Now plummet those babies into the ice water to stop the cooking. After a minute or so, drain the beans and pat dry on a cloth or paper towel.

- Over a medium-veering-on-high heat, melt the butter in a wide frying pan and add the onions. Cook for 3–4 minutes until they are translucent. Chuck in the beans and sauté for another 2–3 minutes before adding all the herbs and some salt and pepper to taste. Stir it all up and cook for 1 more minute. Squeeze over some lemon before serving.

The mash

- Pop the potatoes in a large saucepan and cover with cold water. Salt generously. Bring the water to a rolling boil and keep it going for about 15 minutes. The cubes should be cooked through and tender. Drain and return to the pot.

- Mash the spuds with a – surprise, surprise – potato masher. Try and get it as mashed as humanly possible. Ignore the urge to use a food processor or stick blender. This could activate the starch and make more of a clag glue than a side dish.

- When the mash is positively puréed, pop it back on low to evaporate the last of the water. It should take about a minute or so. Turn the stove off.

- Now begin to add the cubes of butter. Add a couple at a time and stir as they melt. Stir in a little warmed milk. The milk is there to fine-tune the texture. It should be wildly creamy but not runny.

- Season to taste, put a lid on and keep warm while the fish happens.

The fish

- Get a couple of plates warming in a low oven then drink a couple of sizeable glasses of very crisp and cold white wine. This is going to make you feel very classy as you make your very classy French fish.

- With some paper towel, give the fillets a little pat dry on both sides, and because of the wine you're going to mutter to them how nice they look, then season them generously with salt and pepper. Sift the flour onto a dinner plate or baking tray, and dredge both fillets in it, shaking off the excess, and set aside.

- Into a wide non-stick frying pan over medium–high heat whack in the clarified butter to kind of laminate the whole surface of the bottom. When it's shimmering, start to fry one of the fillets skin-side down for somewhere between 2 and 3 minutes then turn her over and fry for another couple of minutes. This will vary by the size of the fillets, but basically both sides should be browned a little and the edges starting to crisp. Remove and place on a warmed plate and then repeat the process with the other fillet.

- Get rid of the oil and give the pan a quick wipe. Add the salted butter and melt over medium heat. Keep it going until it starts to bubble slightly then go brown and, as if you're having a delicious stroke, it'll start to smell a bit nutty. Pop in the capers, shake the pan a little to get them moving but be careful because the butter could rather suddenly seem quite angry and spit at you. It's just acting out and this behaviour has nothing to do with you.

- Turn off the heat and squeeze in the lemon juice before giving the pan another shake. You should be feeling very chefy right now. Also a little drunk. But any time you're shaking a pan you should think *This must be what it's like to be a chef.* Also, when you're doing a lot of cocaine you should think *This must be what it's like to be a chef.*

- Evenly pour the butter sauce over the top of your fillets and sprinkle with parsley and serve absolutely immediately with your mash and beans and do not attempt to have sex afterwards. Too much butter for that.

GOD'S SWEET GIFT TO PAN FRYING – CLARIFIED BUTTER

Clarified butter is a real nice thing to have in the fridge and it will make you feel strong and better than others just knowing it's in there.

It's pretty easy to make, really. Once the milk solids (two terrible words to see next to each other) have been removed from butter, you have yourself some clarified butter. Like ghee, it has a much higher smoke point, but it has a rich, nutty taste so it's perfect for frying fish.

– INGREDIENTS –

Basically, as much unsalted butter as you like, cut into cubes. You can use any amount of butter, but keep in mind that it will reduce as it clarifies. A good rule of thumb (a weird saying) is you generally lose about 20–25 per cent of the volume as you seek clarification.

– METHOD –

- Okay, we're going to start by melting your butter in a heavy saucepan over very low heat. As the butter melts, you'll notice that it starts to separate into three layers: a foamy layer on top, a clear layer in the middle, and a milky layer on the bottom. It's a bit gross.

- Continue to cook the butter on low heat until the foam on top starts to subside and the clear layer in the middle becomes more pronounced. Like dairy carbon dating. This will take about 10–15 minutes.

- Remove the saucepan from the heat and let it cool for a few minutes.

- Get yourself a wooden spoon to skim off the foam from the top and discard it.

- Now pour the clear layer of butter through a fine-mesh strainer or cheesecloth into a clean container. This will remove any remaining milk solids and clarify the butter even further.

- Store the clarified butter in an airtight container in the fridge for up to a month.

SUMMER LOVIN'

It's no secret that Australia is full of some of the world's deadliest animals: spiders, snakes, George Pell. Our harsh climate is up to pussy's bow with things that want us to not be alive anymore. But if I'm honest, as I've grown older I've come to realise it's not the animals that scare me. To be attacked by one of these creatures is really more of an abstract thought than a daily risk. It's the type of tragic thing that happens to other people, like being in a plane crash or becoming a breakfast television host. No, what I truly fear is something much more real. Something significantly more feasible. A confrontation, of any kind, with a Year 9 student. Agile, without responsibility and very, very horny. There is truly no living thing more purpose built for destruction than fifteen-year-old boy.

Throughout my early- to mid-high schooling, my best friend was a boy we'll call Marcus. As a very warm-hearted but at times severe person, Marcus was the type of kid who made other people's parents nervous. With his loose fitting skate shoes, metal shirts and a shelf in his room dedicated to empty cans of Red Bull he was inexplicably keeping, it seemed as though Marc was designed in some corporate lab as a way to research how to sell more Lynx Africa. The anxious and more apprehensive teenagers, the kind of youth I was at that age, tend to attach themselves to personalities like him. The two of us had first become friends around the beginning of high school as Year 7-ers. He was different to the pals I'd had in primary school. More brash and opinionated. He seemed older, somehow. I'd decided he would represent a new era for me. I was going to be different and try being a little more grown up. There was a thrill and what felt like a bit of danger to being around him. With both his parents being diligent shift workers, they were nearly always either asleep or at work. This entitled us to go to his house after school and do pretty much whatever we wanted. Our afternoons and early evenings were filled with the type of busywork boys that age like to dedicate their waking hours to: a dense schedule of setting things on fire, watching *Fight Club* and trying to view images of naked people.

When I was fourteen there were five or six of us in this merry band, but the others had always felt like satellites to me. In my eyes Marcus and I were the closest. Some of my most brain-shaping memories, for better or worse, are from this period in my life. Any time I stayed at his house, which was almost every weekend, there was some reckless adventure to be had. We'd sneak out and just wander around the neighbourhood until the early hours. Him and the rest of our group running ahead of me and egging me on as I called out how I wasn't sure about any of this. It was like characters in an Enid Blyton novel had they been having way more conversations about wanking. The fact I was clearly queer, claiming to be bisexual at the time, in this group of great unwashed straight boys was never even close to an issue, which is frankly bonkers. Sometimes when his older brother and his mates might make a joke at my expense, Marcus was always quick to my rescue by telling him to shut up, often saying, 'Hey, Rhys might be into guys but at least he's not a faggot like you!' We were opposites in so many ways, but for a few years we were inseparable.

Somewhere around the beginning of summer at the tail end of 2004 a few significant things happened. My parents, noticing my interests in animation and filmmaking in general, made the incredibly kind decision to give me a video camera for Christmas. Around the same time, the revelation broke that a house had been condemned down the street from Marcus's place and was due to be demolished. Our gang agreed that while of course we had commiserations for the original occupants, this was some big news for us. As far as we were concerned, we were now homeowners. The place was completely empty, rotting, water damaged and had an enormous backyard entirely overgrown with weeds. It was perfect. It was a clubhouse. Our own secret paradise where we could truly be free. Free to be us. Free to set things on fire and try to look at images of naked people. Any spare moment we had, which was a lot of moments, we met up at our new residence. Day or night we were there trying our first cigarettes and just kind of breaking things. That was a big part of our lives around this time: Smashin'. Shit. Up. With the *Jackass* franchise still going strong in the hearts and minds of teenagers, my camera was regularly used to archive our work. Once, thanks to a serendipitously timed hard rubbish collection, we were able to scour the streets and make a pile of old appliances and small pieces of furniture in one of the rooms, then got to destroying them for no reason as the camera rolled. Gallons upon gallons of hormonal rage poured out the end of hammers and crowbars we'd borrowed from our family sheds. I remember one especially satisfying moment when I got a round of applause for pelting a fax machine so hard at a wall, it lodged itself in there. And there it remained, like some mounted game I'd shot on safari.

That school holiday brought another great move forward for us and our lifestyle. Marcus's family home got the newest object in early-2000s luxury, broadband internet. Our dicks didn't know what hit them. This was a whole new game. We no longer had to rely on our poorly informed imaginations or the underwear section of the Kmart catalogue for sexual inspiration. It was now readily available through a tiny cable coming out of the lounge room wall. At the time my house still had dial-up so a plan was hatched that while at Marc's house, we would look up porn together, which insanely didn't feel weird at the time, and using my camcorder I would film the porn off the computer screen so I could look at it again in private and do my grubby business. I'm not sure what it says about me, but to this day, silently sharing the seat of a computer chair with my best friend in his deserted house as I hold my breath to keep the camera steady and focused on some pixelated people getting absolutely railed is perhaps the most intimate moment of my entire life.

Afterwards we'd drink Milo and watch *Family Guy* as if nothing had ever happened. When I got home I'd quickly hide my special tape by dramatically Blu-Tacking it to the underside of my bedroom desk as if I were a spy hiding microfilm I'd taken of a secret, monstrous weapon. This practice went on for a little while. We were so proud of our system. It made us feel like we were getting away with something. Matters escalated slightly when we returned to school and because of some well-placed brags, I started renting out my camera and grubby mixtape to a couple of friends for a gold coin donation. Marcus and I took requests but it was always agreed we had good taste and deep respect for the craft. It was so much more satisfying than just smashing shit up. We loved the work. Looking back, I was of course 100 per cent in love with him. I always understood nothing would ever happen between us but I just wanted to please him any way possible and I think on some level he knew it but never let it get in the way. We were best buddies. We were business partners.

The porno scheme eventually broke down when on a tear about how messy my room was, my mum began grabbing piles of things out from under my desk. Thanks to all the commotion, with a small clunk my tape fell to the floor and she swiftly picked it up. I could see the cogs turning in her mind. Why was her fourteen-year-old child keeping a videotape stuck under their desk? I have a vivid memory of my mother, tape in hand, sternly asking what in the hell was on it and if I didn't tell her she was just going to have to play it and see. Realising straight away I was cooked whatever I said and truly trying to avoid the severe discomfort of watching my mother watch porn in front of me, I just came clean. I admitted to our racket with the very poorly selected words, 'Fine! It's porn! It's porn I film at Marcus's house!' Her eyes widened to around the size of an affordable family car. This was clearly not what she was expecting to hear. I also hadn't caught the way in which my words could have been misconstrued, so it would be at least another ten minutes before I was able to explain that we were merely documenting premade features and not producing our own. Under the circumstances, this provided some relief, but my insinuation that she should think of it as some sort of archive fell on deaf ears. My generous, naive parents had thought they were opening the doors to the arts when they got me that camera – and in a way they were. But how were they to know they were also raising a professional pornography bootlegger. The camera was confiscated for more than a month, by which point the market had moved on.

Over the next little while things began to change between me and Marcus. A little at first, and then a lot. His parents messily separated and it was all becoming a bit intense at his house. He seemed more intense. Angrier. Rudderless. He was destructive in a more . . . destructive way. By the end of the following summer holiday I'd started to feel like maybe I wasn't fitting in so well in the band anymore. The wacky antics were starting to seem less thrilling and just kind of scarier. He'd started smoking a lot of pot, adding vodka to his Red Bulls and was at times belligerent. A swarm of new friends started hanging out at the clubhouse. They were loose, skipped school and partied like twenty-year-olds. Some of them were older and mean and Marcus just didn't seem as ready to stand up for me anymore. I think I represented a past era for him. Like my primary school friends, I was being left behind. On my last visit to the clubhouse there was a little gathering that turned into a party that escalated to what felt like some sort of coven meeting. Everyone was so out of it and aggressive. Someone pulled my fax machine out of the wall. I kept to myself and missed the good old days when all we did was smash up outdated communication appliances. There must have been a noise complaint or something because all I remember is someone screaming 'Cops!' and everyone scattered like bugs living under a stone. Over the fence, I suddenly found myself careening down the street for blocks and blocks until I ducked down an alleyway. I was puffed, alone and close to tears. I felt out of my depth and incredibly young.

Sometime later, around the same month my family got broadband, the clubhouse was knocked down. A process made far, far easier by the several appliances that had been jammed into load-bearing walls, I expect. It was the end of an era. Marcus and I still spoke at school from time to time, but it was definitely different. For a few years at least. I gradually joined a new group of schoolfriends. They were a more studious, calmer bunch. They represented a different time for me. I was going to be different now.

HOW TO WRITE YOUR FIRST BOOK: PART V

I wonder, will they notice if the font is just a bit bigger?

GOSSIP

I'd never been a political person. Not on purpose, at least. For a long time, newspapers were mainly just the place I found the TV guide. But there comes a point in any minority member's life when you have politics flung onto you. When the subject of marriage equality was going to be voted on in Australia, suddenly like an almond in an açai bowl at a douchey cafe, I was activated.

The process of the plebiscite (a word we had never seen and will probably never see again) was in so many ways absolutely bloody harrowing. It brought up so much anger and gave both sides of the argument space to peddle their worst smears of the other side. When other parts of the world like the UK and the US, with all their socio-political flaws, seemed to have been able to get their shit together and just legalise marriage equality, we just couldn't grasp it. The vote and the way it was handled here just felt so unnecessary. But then finally, after months of grimness, the day arrived for the vote and to hear the results. My fiancé and I decided to head into the city to the front of the State Library of Victoria to watch the announcement. We got the train in. After a few stops it became clear most people around us were going to the announcement because our carriage was just getting gayer and gayer and gayer. So gay. There were signs with fun slogans, shirts with 'Love is Love' plastered across them. People were wearing rainbow flag capes. It was weird because usually when you see a bunch of people wearing flags with signs it's stressful because they are probably about to storm a government building, but this group was quite soothing to look at because it was so gay, as if five stops in we got an arts grant to put on a movement piece for underprivileged teens. Pretty gay train, guys.

And you'd think a train of homos and their friends speeding towards a life-changing moment would be fun, right? It wasn't; we were quite jittery. Veering on scared, even. We were worried about what our country had done. Nervous to discover who Australia really was. Sure, that might sound a little dramatic, and our straight allies would tell us over and over again that they were certain it was going to be okay. *Certain.* When you're in any sort of marginalised group you learn pretty quickly that nothing is ever certain. Because of this, you cling to small victories. Searching for teeny tiny glimmers of decency as you pan through the shit of straight, white, middle-class Australia. This day of reckoning was either going to usher in a new sense for our community that change was possible – that a whole new dawn was breaking – or there was a very real possibility that conservative religious and political leaders were going to be pissing directly onto our faces for the foreseeable future. I mean, look, I love my country. I love Australia with all my heart. But I'm a commie snowflake, so I love Australia in the same way we all love the elderly members of our family. They mean well and they're dear to us, but fucking hell are some of them harbouring some wild, deep, dark 1950s bullshit. You can only chat to your great aunt Joan for twenty minutes before she starts talking about 'them'. And to be honest, we will never have any idea who 'they' are. Neither does she. The months leading up to the vote had shown some of the best, but sadly more so some of the worst, facets of this country. It'd given license for people to spurt out their genuinely troubling views in public with absolute impunity. There were times where it felt like some in the media were picking up a rock and asking the creatures living under it, 'Should we let them?'

'NO!' they would shriek back.

So we're trundling along on the train and people are trying to keep their spirits up and I spy a family across the carriage. Two mothers and their two kids. I could hear one of the mums explaining to the small children what the day had in store. 'Well,' she began, 'we're going to the announcement of some very big news, and if it's a yes we'll shout and cheer and go have a nice lunch somewhere. Now if it's a no, we'll go ten pin bowling.'

That phrase would go on to haunt me for months. I still can't work out if ten pin bowling is a punishment or a reward. I have been bowling twice in my life. Once was for a Christmas party for a retail job I was working at and occasionally shoplifting from. We were waiting in line to pay for our lane when this guy cut in front of me and I was going to say something but then it became clear he'd brought his own bowling shoes. *I'll leave him be,* I thought to myself.

At the State Library, after the results were proclaimed as going our way and the giddiness started to subside among the crowd of thousands, I happened to see the family from the train again. As we strolled past, and with a big smiled pasted on my face, I said loudly, 'Have a nice lunch!' The mothers looked at me, having no idea what I meant and smiled the way you do so when someone on drugs is trying to strike up a conversation.

Getting married had never really entered my mind. When it's not ever really presented as a possibility, you go around pretending it's not something you want. But suddenly, years before the vote, for no reason in particular, I decided I wanted to marry Kyran. Now, when I say 'no reason in particular' I don't mean it was without reason – the guy's a keeper. I guess what I mean is that there just wasn't any enormous epiphany. No huge ah-ha moment brought on by some romantic act. The thought of spending the rest of my life with him didn't occur to me as we, say, strolled through a garden or swam in a lake or looked into each other's eyes as we jerked each other off in a gondola. Nothing as lovey-dovey as that. It was simple: during the peak of summer we were quite hungover in our tiny, sticky apartment in the inner west of Sydney and as we crossed one another in the hallway he grabbed me, squeezed me, kissed me on the neck and suggested we order burgers for lunch. BAM! It hit me like a tonne of beef. At that moment I suddenly couldn't imagine not wanting to be with him. I just couldn't. I was unable to fathom a situation where I wouldn't be happy with him. I saw our lives ahead of us. Decades upon decades of him ordering me burgers as I continued emotionally blackmailing him into staying with me. You know, being in a relationship.

So now I knew it. I was going to ask him to marry me. I knew the why, but now I had to work out the how. This was already going to be a problem because I am not the gift-giver in our relationship. Every couple has someone who is very good at presents, and someone who sweatily hands over the gift while saying sorry. The more I thought about it, the more I realised I really shouldn't be the one proposing because I already knew I was going to overthink it, get myself into a tizzy and do some weird shit where I organised a hot air balloon ride that we parachute from to land on horses we then ride down the beach, or some shit. We'd be up there in the balloon and I'd try and do it and he'd say no and then we'd just have to aimlessly drift in the sky with the guy driving the balloon. Jesus Christ, my chest was getting tight thinking about it. Maybe there was something to be said for simply jerking him off in a gondola?

At least one thing was crystal clear, it would not be in a public place in front of a whole bunch of people. Why do people do that? I mean, anyone who has decided they are going to propose will know it's a bizarre feeling. It's hard to explain the sensation. You have this little secret you're carrying around in your chest, as if you have really, really good gossip. Everything inside is telling you to blurt it out all the time to anyone you meet. Having experienced this feeling, I understand the instinct of very public proposals. I do. But let's be honest with ourselves, only a true, grand high fuckhead follows that instinct to completion. Why would you think anyone outside your immediate family would give two shits about who you want to marry? You see those insane viral videos of people's extravagant set-ups. Sky writing, trained animals, drones, a personal appearance from Hilary Duff singing the theme to *Lizzie McGuire*. And the victim in all of this? The proposee. What are they meant to think of it all? Is this the norm now? Is this a full lifetime of oversharing and the dissection of the most significant, private topics of their existence? If they say yes will they have to spend the rest of time looking over their shoulder in fear that some uncomfortable, huge romantic gesture is about to happen? What a boner shrinker.

And what happens if it doesn't go your way? I was once serving my country as a performer on a budget cruise ship. Sometimes these types of gigs can be dreamy and sometimes they are like performing at an RSL, when they're just whacking something onstage for people to see while they have a rest from the pokie machines, bottomless Bundy Cokes and the vastest sneeze-guarded buffet you'll ever see in your life. A highlight for me on these trips is the *Gong Show*-style talent contest where passengers can get up on stage and try their hand at stand-up for the first time in front of a big audience. The comics sit at the front as a panel of judges, and of course the best part is that one of us is sitting at a gong and when things get too shit, as it almost always does, we gong them. Then one by one we give feedback. It's raucous, brutal and incredibly cathartic.

This particular day I was manning the gong. It hadn't been too wild, really: a few fresh divorcees ticking something off the bucket list, a couple of tweens recounting rude jokes their dads had told them, and one elderly widow making a lot of jokes that made us start to believe she had probably helped her husband die. The usual. The host announced the last performer. A man in his late fifties took to the stage. He was a big guy, white with slightly sun-damaged skin and the high level of self-confidence that made me think he probably owns a store that makes built-in wardrobes and other storage systems. I can't remember, but it would be a safe bet to say his name was Darryl. He struggled at first to take the microphone out of the stand and began the conventional approach these guys take to comedy. They kind of uncomfortably strut around and recite joke-book jokes and when it gets a groan they will inevitably say, 'Well, it was funnier in the shower.' After about two minutes the crowd was getting restless and I was pretty close to gonging him out when quite suddenly Darryl changed the mood. He said, 'Now look, before you gong me off, I just have to say this. I don't have any mother-in-law jokes because I don't have one. But I'd like to change that.' A flurry of excitement gushed over the crowd. He then proceeded to bring up a woman to the stage. I want to say her name was Donna. Darryl got on one knee and flat-out asked her to marry him. The crowd went absolutely bananas. People were getting their phones out and filming. We couldn't believe this was happening. No matter how this cruise had been we would always have the story that we saw that nice suburban couple get engaged in open water. The audiences calmed down and we waited for her 'yes'.

There was a pause. Like, a long pause. It wasn't so much a pregnant pause, but more that the pause had had the baby and wasn't quite coping. Donna's body language was retracting. With the microphone too close to his mouth, our new favourite comedian/performance artist muttered 'please'. More phones started filming. 'The divorce isn't even final yet,' the front row heard her reply. The pause continued. Donna was now on her way to being about the size of a marble. I didn't know where to look and as my eyes darted around the theatre I saw my hand and the soft mallet I was holding in it. It's at this point I made a call. I'm not proud of it but there just didn't seem like any way out. I just . . . well, I gonged him. Hundreds of people were on that ship to gamble, but I think it's safe to say no one had lost so much from a bet as Darryl.

So no, a public proposal was out of the question. After thinking about it I'd come to the conclusion it should just be between me and Kyran. That way if we found ourselves in a Darryl and Donna situation, no one had to know about it and I could do what's expected, which is, wander out into the ocean in a wedding dress and leave a note blaming Kyran. Like a grown-up.

On a Saturday a couple of weeks after I'd made the decision, I still hadn't come up with a plan. We were coming up to Christmas and I thought maybe I'd just wait until the new year. The thinking was *This isn't something to rush into. The moment will make itself known.* The first thing to do was find a ring and then the rest would come naturally. Right? That afternoon we were headed to the wedding of one of our closest friends and I made a little plan to see if I could maybe steal a conversation with the groom at his most loved-up and perhaps ask him for any advice about nailing the proposal. The wedding and reception were one of those events where everything was just right. I knew almost everyone there, the ceremony itself was super short and the couple were both from wealthy Greek families so there were delicious meats and I was allowed to smash plates. That's really all I want at the end of the day.

Kyran was at the time working in weekend breakfast radio and had to be at work the next morning at 5 am, so we decided we would hang out for a bit but definitely not have a big, late one. I was also going through a little bit of a period of trying not to drink as much. Not to be good to myself, but more to the people around me. As they were about the start the speeches, champagne was being passed around. *Well, it's rude not to have a champagne for the toasts*, I bargained to myself. *I'll have one. One!* Nine. I'm told I had nine champagnes during the speeches. Then some ouzo. After the toasts I apparently just kept saying to everyone what a beautiful wedding it was. Over and over. The bride, elderly relatives, the guy cutting up the lamb. Lots of big hugs from your ol' pal drunk Rhys happening all over the shop. I could feel the engagement bubbling up in my ribs.

In the bathroom while washing my hands I looked in the mirror and said quietly to myself, 'You're gonna try and get engaged. Shhhhhh.' Then I gave a big smile to the man at the sink next to me and wandered out. At around midnight when Kyran found me standing at a window gently swaying, it was time to go home. He loaded me into the back of an Uber. 'Fantastic wedding. Wasn't that a fucking beautiful wedding?' By the time we got back to the house he had to be on air in four hours, so he loaded me into bed and gave me my weed vape to tranquilise me like an escaped zoo animal. This is where my memory gets a little fuzzy. Piecing together my recollection as well as the bits and bobs I've subsequently been told, it seems the night's final event went like this: after a few minutes of peace, Kyran was lying there with his eyes and entire body clenched tight, trying desperately to go to sleep. I started up again. 'Just such a beautiful wedding,' I muttered.

'Mhmm. Yep. Gotta go to sleep now, okay?' my beloved replied with fast disappearing patience. But I persisted. I needed him to know just how beautiful this wedding was. I didn't think he understood the gravity of it. 'It was just, just, like . . . just beautiful.'

'Shhhhhhhh.' He was at the end of his rope and ready to use it to strangle me.

I'm there sprawled out, still half-dressed in my suit with vape billowing out of me as if I'm some ill-advised, MA15+ *Thomas the Tank Engine* character, when I have this moment of clarity. Through all the booze and Greek meat and clouds of THC I have an epiphany. This is the moment I've been waiting for.

'It was a good wedding wasn't it?'

'Rhys, please just—'

I cut him off. 'Shush shush shush. Listen. It was a good wedding and I was just wondering . . . would you do that also?'

There is a long pause of silence. Not Donna and Darryl long, but long enough to be stressful.

I hear him clear his throat, 'Excuse me. What did you say?'

'I said, "Would you do that also?"'

In a jolt, the bedside lamp goes on and Kyran sits up. 'I'm sorry, are you asking me to marry you?'

I take a drag and sit up as my eyes adjust. 'Yeah. Weeeeeee!'

'Well,' as his eyes narrow, 'if you're going to ask me to marry you, you need to actually ask me to marry you.'

I am instantaneously irate with him for not getting this. 'Fine!' I cry out. 'Will you fucking marry me!'

The next morning he got back from work and had to tell me what had happened.

Later that year Kyran and I found ourselves in Scotland for the

Edinburgh Fringe Festival. I was tried and lazy and was spending most daylight hours in the apartment conserving my energy for the late nights of shows and partying. For days he'd been trying to get me to go for a walk with him up Arthur's Seat, a well-known hiking track up a hill with stunning views of the city. He wasn't giving up so I conceded and began lugging myself towards the track. I was so annoyed to be doing it, I really leant into passive-aggressively huffing and puffing and giving two-word answers to any and all of his questions as he tried to make cheerful conversation. We're walking and walking and walking and close to the peak we stop at this little cliff bit. We look out to what is undeniably a phenomenal view. A wide-open vista with the greens of the Scottish countryside flowing into the striking architecture of a wildly old city. It was very nice, but I was in the type of mood that meant I didn't want him to know I thought it was nice. I'm a real gift. Kyran placed his backpack on the ground and asked if I wanted some water.

'Sure,' I mumbled as I turned away. I heard the bag unzip and some rustling. When I turned back, there was Kyran. On one knee, holding a match box.

I took a deep breath. 'There's a fucking ring in there, isn't there?'

He smiled wide and nodded.

'Fuck, you are competitive.'

Of course, my mood changed in an instant, I said yes and he slipped the perfectly lovely gold wedding band onto my finger. We sat down at the top of the hill and took in the view before starting our way back down together. It had gone well, so we went for a nice lunch and did not have to go bowling.

HERBAL

I've been told by my fine publishing pals at Penguin Random House that it might not be a very good idea to say anything in this comedy book that could point to the fact I have ever taken part in any kind of illegal activities. I didn't even ask. They just kind of brought it up out of nowhere. They warned me that a passing mention of casual recreational drug use could potentially leave myself, as well as them, vulnerable to possible litigation in the future as well as make getting international work visas tough for me.

With all this being said, please believe me when I say this section is all completely imagined. It's what I imagine it would be like had I ever consumed a drug not prescribed by a doctor and then given to me by a licensed chemist. I have a very good imagination, you see. I can just do some simple Google searches on the side effects and really get into the experience to explain what it would have been like if since about, oh, I don't know, let's say, seventeen years old I had taken part in a whole myriad of recreational drug use. Uppers mainly. Ecstasy, speed, coke, speed you think is coke, a fun mystery item my friend found on the ground of a gay bar that we took in a bathroom stall while crossing our fingers, wishing one another luck and waving goodbye to each other just in case. But of course I haven't done any of that. I'm a good girl. Okay, cool. We're covered, right? Great, let's move on.

In the last few years, as I leave my roaring twenties behind, I've really started getting into downers. Drugs, I mean. Not a sad story about a fire in an aged care home or something. I mean anything that for a certain amount of time will make me even slightly less clear of where, who and why I am. For as long as I can remember, I have always been a hugely highly strung person. Sleep is a big problem for me. I didn't notice it until recently, but I was never able to grab onto anything close to a full night's rest. You notice this in your thirties. When I was younger, I loved uppers. It started in my late teens when in Newcastle my friends and I would buy very cheap and shitty ecstasy and run around fields in semi-rural areas. The whole thing was very innocent and you could never describe me as addled in any way, but there was definitely a time when I much preferred being awake. Very, very awake for quite long periods of time. I suppose I used to want to be aware. Not about anything in particular. Just like, open to everything. For many people, our late teens and early twenties are a stage of life where we feel this intense FOMO for absolutely all things. We just want to know about it, whatever it is, in its entirety, all the time. And if we don't know about it, we'll pretend we do. Then, as you drift into the next decade and begin to actually learn about life, you quickly realise you really don't want to know about any of it. It is all just a bit much. This moment heralds the first rumbles of that anxiety disorder every living person above the age of twenty-nine develops but doesn't tell anyone about. You say to yourself, 'I'd like to know a bit less about all of these things, please. That would be nice. And maybe a nice long nap would be good? Yes. People are always saying how important sleep is so I'll have a little nigh-nighs and I'll feel better.' So you get into bed ready for your sleep and just before you drift off, you're newly wise-to-the-world brain decides that this is definitely the perfect time to show you a list it's been compiling of every mistake you've ever made. Think of it as a sort of highlights reel, spanning more than thirty years, of your regrets, your failures and your deepest fears. Perhaps something as simple as that day in the third grade when you called your teacher 'Mum'. Or like that day in the third grade when you called your mum by your teacher's name. Enter from stage left, downers. Nothing too heavy, don't panic! Not proper prescription pills or anything like that – I'm not talking about *chemical* things. You're never going to see the headline QUEER COMEDIAN WHO'S OFTEN CONFUSED FOR ONE OF THE OTHER ONES ACCIDENTALLY OVERDOSES ON A COCKTAIL OF BENZOS, HALLUCINOGENS AND MELATONIN GUMMIES. No, thank you. Not for me. I mean just a little somethin' somethin', usually in the form of a vape before bedtime that just takes the edge off things. And by 'things' I mean 'being alive' and by 'edge' I mean being 'completely conscious of the fact that that I'm alive'.

I've come to respect and enjoy weed later than most, but not a moment too soon. Mine is a classic tale in which I tried it once in my teens and had a terrible time so was put off for ages. My first experience was for the same reason most gay teenage boys try things: to impress a group of attractive straight males. In my case, a cluster of unkempt sk8ter bois at an out-of-control house party my best friend had while her family was away. We must have all been about sixteen and the fellas were sitting in a circle in the backyard. I'd had a couple of Midori Illusions so was really feeling myself and decided to join the fold. I was welcomed in and began to feel like Jane Goodall. We couldn't quite understand each other, but through some rudimentary sign language it became clear one of the guys, who was more side fringe than person, was asking if I'd like a hit. Having never had a whiff of the stuff in my life, I determined it would be totally fine to take three enormous toots off a bong. For those of you unaware of the magnitude of this decision, it's kind of like if you were feeling a bit chilly, and instead of popping on a light sweater, you just covered your body in petrol and then set yourself on fire. Within seconds everything began to spin. I was starting to 'green out'. I remember thinking that my body had started to feel very tight, while the world felt quite loose. I must have blacked out because I came to in the bathroom with my bestie holding my head over the toilet as the entire contents of my insides came roaring out of my head. I'd completely forgotten we'd spent the afternoon eating cherries, so when I looked into the bowl and saw red, fleshy chunks I looked up at my pal and asked meekly through tears if I was dying. She was a bit stoned herself so in a teenager's attempt to be deep she replied, 'Rhys, we're all dying.' This didn't help my situation and I began to sob uncontrollably. She tucked me up in her brother's empty bed and the next morning when I awoke in nothing but my underwear, curled up in a SpongeBob SquarePants sheet with red stains around my mouth, I vowed never to touch weed again.

A while ago I made a conscious decision to make a genuine attempt to think about maybe looking into my 'consumption habits', and at the very least curb the quantity of uppers I was doing. Again, I wasn't being a maniac about it. If I was at a party or hanging out after a gig, though, if someone offered me a little sniff of something, sure, I'd have a bump. And if no one had offered me any, I'd stand around the people who I figured probably had some until they did. You know, just being friendly. My turning point to the sleepier side of things came when a few years back a close friend had his thirtieth birthday party at a school camp. The expansive site, complete with a mess hall and a dozen or so cabins with bunk beds, was closed for the season and some lovely, way too trusting old man made the terrible mistake of allowing over a hundred rapidly ageing queers to take over the whole place for twenty-four hours. It was chaos. I have never seen so much drug use in my life. There was no secrecy about it because we were in the middle of nowhere and everyone was doing it. It felt like the first thirty-five minutes of a 1979 slasher movie. A few hours later, some drag queens arrived to perform. I recall hearing one of them exclaiming before the show, 'Jesus Christ, these homos are fucking off their faces.' That's a real big red flag, in retrospect. Do you know how wildly off the rails you need to be to shock a professional drag entertainer into a double take? It must have been like performing to a room of the type of people you stopped being friends with a decade ago because they're always double-fisting drinks and trying to start arguments with bouncers. I was suddenly a little too aware.

I must make it clear that I am very much against the likes of children doing drugs, blah blah blah. But it's always been interesting to me that I made the snap decision to never do weed again after one bad time, yet stuck to my guns with the countless other vices I'd experimented with, often with similarly dreadful outcomes. I'll never not find it hilarious that Australia has the reputation around the world as being this laidback, larrikin society of hot beachgoers and people telling other people that isn't a knife. Most of us know better than that. We are a twitchy bunch of people down here. Anyone who isn't, oh, I don't know, straight, male, white and rich, will appreciate that as soon as you scratch just beneath the surface of this country's unperturbed vibe lays a bonkers Rube Goldberg machine of tense social violence. The truth is, if you're white, you might not even be aware pot is illegal. But in grim and completely not shocking news, if say, for example, you're an Indigenous Australian who gets caught with a little dime bag of weed in certain areas of this country, there's statistically an 80 per cent chance you'll end up in court. I mean, fucking hell. 'Cos *that* seems like the right thing to be pumping a bunch of energy into. Think of the resources we'd save by not needlessly overburdening our legal system with a steaming pile of racially motivated charges. I tell you what, it's pretty bloody hard to die in custody if you're not in custody.

We don't like new ideas around here. Or anything that we don't completely understand or relate to on a personal level. Gambling, alcohol, improv. These are all completely legal pastimes that when abused can have detrimental effects on your life and the people around you. But no, pot is a threat to the fabric of the country. At the moment, the estimated annual social cost attached to booze in Australia sits somewhere around $66.8 billion, whereas each year $1.7 billion of taxpayer's money is spent on ganja-related law enforcement. The financial and personal damage improv can cause is of course, immeasurable.

WILDLY BASIC BIG NATURALS COOKIES . . . NOTHING TO SEE HERE

During one of the long lockdowns we enjoyed in my hometown of Melbourne amid that tiny catastrophic global health crisis we had a few years ago, I made a rather large batch of the dough from the below recipe and froze individuals balls so each and every night I could bake a fresh cookie.

– SERVES: TWELVE –

– PREPARATION TIME: TWENTY MINUTES –

– COOKING TIME: FIFTEEN MINUTES –

– INGREDIENTS –

120 g completely normal unsalted butter
that has nothing else going on

100 g white sugar

165 g brown sugar

1 tsp salt

1 egg

1 tsp vanilla extract
155 g plain flour
½ tsp baking soda
1½ cups peanut M&Ms

– METHOD –

- In a saucepan, on a very, very low heat, melt the butter. Do not microwave it. Just don't, okay? It could make the butter . . . not good anymore.

- Get yourself a big ol' bowl and whisk together the sugars, melted butter and salt until you get a sort of gross looking paste. Whisk in the egg and vanilla, beating until light ribbons fall off the whisk and remain for a short while before dissolving back into the mixture.

- Sift in the flour and baking soda, then fold into the mixture with a spatula. Fold in the M&Ms, then chill the dough for at least 30 minutes, but overnight can give it a slightly more caramelly flavour.

- Preheat the oven to 160°C fan-forced (180°C conventional). Some recipes for cookies will say hotter than that. That might work for them but with this one the temperature needs to be low. Bake these babies too hot and fast and the cookies will be . . . not good anymore. Line a baking sheet with baking paper.

- Using a dessert spoon, scoop the dough into balls about the size of an ice cream scoop onto the baking paper-lined tray. Try and space them out to about 8 or 10 cm apart and about 5 cm from the edge.

- Bake for 15–20 minutes, or until the edges have started to barely brown. Cool completely before serving. Eat half and see how you feel after a bit. Later on you may feel very hungry. Do not under any circumstances eat another one of these cookies to get rid of this hunger. Enjoy!

HUMAN RESOURCES

I think we can all agree, jobs aren't good. People say things such as, 'If you find a job you love, you'll never work a day in your life.' Well, I tell you what, I have always wanted to write a book. It's been a fantasy for a long, long time. The very idea of having something on the shelves with my name on it is unreal. Right now, at this very second, I am living my dream. And to be honest, it's been a real hassle.

You first job is exciting. Maybe you're fourteen and nine months, a deeply strange and specific age for the government to choose as the legal age of work in Australia. I remember thinking how grown-up it felt to get a job. I was excited at the very notion that I'd be part of a community, the workforce. I'd have a tax file number, I'd have lunch breaks and form bonds with my co-workers. You have this sensation you are somehow now a more valid member of society. Then you do that first shift on the first day and wander out thinking to yourself, *Well, how can I never do anything like that ever again in my whole life?*

That's been my continuing energy when it comes to the workforce. I may have had a bunch of jobs, but I would say I've worked a total of four or maybe five hours in my life.

I've worked in a few restaurants, fast food, retail. I used to think of myself as a real people person, back when I was starting out. It was at a discount variety store, the type of depressing place where the staff appear startled to see any customers. All the products seem familiar, but something is slightly off. In the toy section there was no Barbie or Ken dolls. Instead we sold the Tina doll. Tina had wild eyes, a smile that told a sad story and she came complete with mobile phone, pink laptop and an outfit that looked as if she was borrowing her housemate's pantsuit for yet another job interview she knew she wouldn't get. I knew I should finish up at that discount store for two reasons. Firstly, the products at the store started to make some sense to me. Secondly, I was fired. I was found in the one corner of the store at which the cameras weren't pointed, fast asleep on a pile of budget dog beds. I was asked to hand in my name badge and my pricing gun, like some sort or morally flexible but emotionally misunderstood detective in a gritty crime drama.

These days I'm often nervous to reveal what I do for work. These days whenever I'm in a situation where I must sit with a stranger for an extended period of time such as an in an Uber, on a flight or while filling out a police report, the conversation will almost always come to what I do for a living. Without fail, I will lie. Not enormous lies. Just a slight meandering around the truth. Sometimes I'll say I'm in TV production. It's vague and usually people tend not to want to know what that means. For many years I said I worked in retail and depending on my mood or how drunk I was, I would go on to tell a rather intricate story about how I'm managing this store and it's mostly fine but 'I recently hired my cousin and I think she's stealing cash from the till. I just don't know what to do about it because they are family and have had a rough go of it lately, but this is my job on the line, too.' If I got it just right, usually there were no follow-on questions and, if anything, a deathly silence reigned from then on. Sometimes you have to make your own fun, you know?

The reason I never casually tell people I'm a comedian is because it just never goes the way you want it to. They will ask me to tell them a joke, I will as politely as possible decline, then without fail and as very bluntly as they can, the new friend will tell me they have never heard of me and go on to list the comedians they have heard of. In my business, if someone has not heard of you, they automatically think you are not successful and, potentially, delusional. They jump straight to pity. 'Hey good for you.' Most people don't really know what the actual job is so they automatically think they could do it as well. It's like writing. They'll let anyone write a book these days. It's ridiculous.

No one likes to admit it, but corporate work is the grimy, crooked little backbone of nearly the entire entertainment industry, especially in Australia. Comedians and musicians would love you to think we are plodding along nicely on hopes, dreams and artistic integrity, but unfortunately hopes and dreams don't pay bills and the only thing artistic integrity ever got anyone was some weird cryptic sentence in their eulogy like 'They always played to the beat of their own drum', which is just a nice way of saying you were a bit of work to be around. Even the most wide-brimmed hat wearing, self-published guitar-stroking Byron bae has a set list of Joss Stone covers she can whack out at a moment's notice so executives in badly decorated event spaces can slow dance with a colleague and afterwards offer the artist indispensable advice like, 'You should try and get a song on the radio.'

I once had a corporate gig where I was flown to Far North Queensland to host a two-day seminar for around three hundred regional store managers of a certain large-scale fast-food chain. You know the one. The main one. Whenever you arrive at this type of hosting engagement, no matter how big or small, you are always immediately told straight away by someone about who hosted it last year, what a great job they did and how they tried to get them again this time but unfortunately that person was unavailable. So they had to get you. I've started to think it's a tactic. They are negging me into doing a good job because apparently last year a more successful person had better interpersonal skills. I tell you what: it works. I suddenly go from carefree mistress with a paid-for condo in the city to the new wife of a widower trying desperately to connect with his kids. When I got to the resort where the conference was being held I was told I was allowed to swear and basically say whatever I wanted as long as I didn't speak about the company in a negative way or their competition outlets in the positive. This is not unusual at these types of gigs. I was sat at a table with three of the upper echelon executives of the Australian arm of the company and was fascinated to find out that every single one of them had begun working instore in their teens. They'd begun their journey in the company with mops, hairnets and a modest staff discount, and now they had enormous offices in a skyscraper and, I'd imagine, all the hash browns they can eat. Over the next couple of days, what struck me was just how horny for their jobs everyone was. It was wild. Cult-like, almost. At one point, one of the speakers mentioned another multinational, specialising in mostly chicken, was beating them in the sale of chicken burgers and that something was going to have to be done to fix that before the next quarter. After she'd finished I got up on stage and before announcing it was time for a tea break I figured I'd take a little risk within the parameters of being allowed to swear, so I announced that speaking personally, 'I reckon all these chicken places can just fuck off,' and continued with, 'I say we just go burn them down to the ground.' I delivered this purely expecting a little bit of a laugh and maybe some furrowed brows from management. That wasn't to be. What I got was an eruption from the crowd of such terrifying proportions that it genuinely felt like maybe we were about to head down to the rag, glass bottle and petrol store before getting to work firebombing some chicken shops.

The most common question I'll be asked about my job is if I get hecklers. I will now answer that here. No, not really. It's not actually much of a thing. Oh sure, it happens from time to time but I wouldn't call it a hazard of the job. It does strike me that stand-up is one of the few performance art forms where audience members shouting out something appears to be acceptable, and even applauded. I don't want to be a little baby about it but no one's heckling ballet. No one is chatting among themselves or calling out over the sound of the first violin during the symphony. I've never been at a bad production of *Death of a Salesman* and heard someone shout from the back, 'Die already!'

I will genuinely never understand the purpose of heckling. Not once have I ever been an audience member and thought to myself, *Yeah, everyone here wants to know what I think of this.* The problem is, when people do it, it's usually in the heat of the moment so what they say can be weird, or at times ugly. It's for a very similar reason I've never sent a picture of my penis to anyone. The rare heckler who finds themselves arcing up is usually under the impression it's part of the performer's job to have a chat to them, so they think they're helping. They aren't, of course, but for the most part it's not too bothersome. It just tends to be someone who's drunk trying to be part of the show. On most occasions you can say something about their job, their mother or their face and they will shut up because the audience clapped. However it never ceases to amaze me when that same person who disrupted the show and angered the rest of the audience will approach me afterwards, Bundy in hand, and be all, 'That was me! I was the heckler! Wasn't it funny!' No, sir. No, it was not.

I suppose it used to be a lot more common. In the early days a heckle would shatter me. Someone would yell something and I'd go way too hard too soon and say some pretty whack shit in reply. Although strangely it's not the loud ones that hurt. Someone booming that I am not funny doesn't get to me. It's the quiet ones. The stealth missiles that only you can hear. The near-silent attacks that travel into your ears and bounce around your soul for a few days. At the very beginning of my career I was performing a show somewhere near Bondi Beach in Sydney. The gig was the type that's thrown together by a pub because they think people want to watch something like comedy while they eat their meals. They don't. They do not want to see an angry little redhead talking into a karaoke machine. They just want to eat their schnitties in peace. I was still working in retail and I'd been booked to do twenty minutes on stage. There were going to be two problems with that. I probably had about ten minutes of material at the most and there was no stage, just four tables pushed together in the corner and an apple box as a step. With only about fifteen people in a bistro that could fit two hundred, as the host was bringing me on he completely forgot my name and just confidently made one up as close as possible. Ryan Nichols. I get up there and without hesitation start bombing. Like, beautifully bombing. Even crickets would be too uncomfortable to say anything. There I was on stage, drowning in the silence when I heard an elderly woman near the front say ever so quietly to her equally geriatric husband, 'I think I've seen enough of whatever this person it trying to do.' They then rose to their feet and shuffled slowly past me and out the door. Poor Ryan Nichols. A true death of a salesman.

The weirdest heckle I ever received wasn't from a person at all. I was performing at an RSL. RSLs are an important part of the Australian performer ecosystem. You perform in them on the way up and then again on the way down. I knew it was going to be an interesting night because as I entered the lobby, a very old man looked at me, grabbed me by the shoulders and said into my face, 'Fuck, you're different.' I don't think he meant anything by it. Just said the things he saw. The show started to a pretty packed room of lovely rural people and it was fine. Not amazing, but not horrible. We were getting away with it and not a torch or pitchfork was in sight. Now I didn't know this, but in some RSLs they do this thing where every few hours they play The Last Post. Everyone in the building takes a moment to remember the fallen, then gets back to the pokies and schooner + parma combos. Later I would be told they usually turn off the speakers that play this song when there's a show going on in the performance space. On this particular night someone had forgotten so about three minutes into my set a speaker at the back of the room started blaring a voice that repeated the phrase 'Please stand and face east' three times. For the first two times everyone was rather confused. I for one thought I had lost my mind or my pill had kicked in early. By the third repeat the 400 people in the audience rose to their feet and faced east. Then, for let's say four full minutes, a room full of people at a comedy show stood in silence and remembered fallen soldiers. At the end they all sat down and stared at me. All I could think of saying was, 'I think we can definitely say I will never fucking forget that.'

DEEP FRIED HAND PIES NOT IN ANY WAY CONNECTED TO A LARGE FAST-FOOD CHAIN

The Golden Arches have always and will always be my grease trap of choice. I'm sorry, but there just isn't any competition. Sure, the burgers are fine or whatever, the fries can sometimes be damp, but who cares because in my opinion the true jewel in the clown's crown is the simple pleasure that is their apple pie. It's my hero. When I grow up I want to be a McDonalds apple pie. On a menu chock-a-block full of spongy mystery textures, the crisp and flaky deep-fried pie exists in a class of its own. It's as if it were sent from the future to save my meal, from somewhere new and foreign yet with the power to bring on a sense of acute nostalgia . . . Capitalism. It feels like good, clean capitalism.

This recipe for homemade fried apple pies is simple enough to make, though the quantity of sugar, butter and delicious fried dough isn't going to win you any prizes at the World Health Awards for Best Healthiness. I've made it a bunch of times and the reaction is always the same. People lose their minds. I've experimented with different fillings like blueberries and mixed berries and they were great, but I just keep coming back to the classic apple. This is a great one if ever you're asked to bring over a dessert to someone's house and want to be a bit camp and kitsch. They are easy to prepare at home and then fry up at your friend's house. Then you don't have to deal with getting rid of a vat of used oil. Or the smell of a vat of boiling oil.

You could absolutely make your own puff pastry if you have a spare entire day. I've done it before and I'll do it again. Personally I think homemade pastry, especially puff, is to be used on something showy and beautiful, like a tarte tatin or Portuguese tarts. In my experience, making your own is 30 per cent for you own satisfaction and 70 per cent holding it over people so they know you are just a little bit better than them. Real friends don't care. One of the most underhanded things you can do to the host of a dinner party is ask if they made their own pastry.

– SERVES: FOUR –

– PREPARATION TIME: CLOSE TO AN HOUR –

– COOKING TIME: ABOUT TWENTY MINUTES –

– INGREDIENTS –

2 sheets of some regular store-bought puff pastry

Filling

3 medium granny smith apples (or similar firm, acidic apples), peeled, cored and cut into 1.5ish cm chunks

½ packed cup white sugar

½ packed cup brown sugar

2 tbsp unsalted butter, melted

juice half a lemon (about 1½ tbsp)

2 tsp vanilla paste

1½ tsp ground cinnamon

1 tsp ground ginger

½ tsp allspice

½ tsp fine sea salt

1 tbsp cornflour dissolved in 2 tbsp water

Cinnamon sugar

⅔ cup white sugar

2 tsp cinnamon

½ tsp garam masala

Some good quality vanilla bean ice cream, to serve

– METHOD –

- Pop the apples and sugars into a medium saucepan and stir until completely coated. Set aside for about 20 minutes.

- Place the pan over a medium–high heat and add the butter, lemon juice, vanilla, cinnamon, ginger, allspice and salt and then mix together and bring to a rolling boil, stirring occasionally until most of the liquid has evaporated and the apples are tender but not mushy (about 8 minutes). Turn off the heat and stir in the cornflour slurry until it's all thick and glossy in there. Set aside until completely cooled.

- Once the filling has cooled, slice both sheets of pastry into four equal strips and separate them. Using your fingies, ever so slightly wet the edges of each and spoon about two tablespoons of the filling onto the upper half of the pastry strips. Fold the bottom half over the top, run your wet fingers around the edge and then seal all the way around by pressing the edges together with a fork. Does that make sense? You know what I mean, right?

- Transfer the pies onto a tray and refrigerate for at least 15 minutes to firm up. Take them out just before frying.

- Heat the oil in a deep fryer to 180°C, or fill a heavy pot or wok with about 5–7 cm of vegetable oil and use a kitchen thermometer to check it heats to 180°C.

- While the oil heats, whisk together the cinnamon sugar ingredients in a wide mixing bowl and set aside

- When the oil is at 180°C, working in batches of two or three at a time, fry the pies for around 2 minutes on each side until they are browned and look very bad for you. Remove and pop them on some paper towel for a few seconds then straight into the cinnamon sugar and toss until coated. Serve immediately. People are gonna lose it.

LOVE ALL

In a disappointing circumstance of living up to the stereotype, sport just ain't for me. Not from a lack of trying. I've given it a go, ever since early childhood attempts on an under-10s soccer team when my dad was our coach and found himself in a constant battle to remind me that what we were wearing were called uniforms and not costumes. Then a few years later my request to try gymnastics was revealed as a ploy to just get my hands on one of those ribbons I'd seen them twirling in the 2000 Sydney Olympics. And finally in more recent times my partner takes me to a bevy of sporting events and finds himself in a constant battle to remind me that what they are wearing are called uniforms and not costumes.

I grew up in city obsessed with the incredibly brutal athletic performance of Rugby League. For many it was like a religion. Houses were painted in the team colours. When the Newcastle Knights beat the Manly Eagles in the 1997 Grand Final, I still remember how it felt like the entire city had erupted. There was partying and utter chaos in the streets as if they/we had not only put a ball over a line quite a few times in a row, but had also just dethroned a fascist regime. The players of our victorious Knights team were lorded as gods who wandered among us raising our spirits and only very occasionally punching a bouncer. That is until they stopped playing, of course. Then they were just men again. Men so badly beaten they looked like ninja turtles who's lost their shells. I remember once a star of the game announced he was retiring following close to fifteen years on the field. After that amount of time you'd imagine an X-ray of his skull would look like a spiderweb. At the end of his final game he received an incredible farewell in front of thousands of adoring fans at Newcastle stadium. They hooted and hollered as he left the field while waving goodbye and fighting back tears. Where was he going, we all wondered? Some higher plane where the forces of gravity are different so bone density doesn't matter so much? Three months later he turned up to my high school to fix the slushy machine. A completely valid way to earn a crust, but undeniably a different world. When he was done, he limped across the quad carrying his tools to his car and I saw our canteen lady eyeing him from a distance. She scrunched up her nose, leant her shoulder against a wall and said to a volunteer mother, 'Sad, isn't it? They fall so far.' The mum shrugged and they both got back to work – the making of over one hundred terrible sandwiches.

I have tried to show interest in competitive physical activities but I've come to believe I don't have it in me to care. I need to be clear that in no way do I think I'm above them. Not the athletes themselves, at least – they're amazing. Though there are some sports fans, and I mean only some, that I think we can all agree are essentially oxygen thieves. My favourite is when a team of some sort wins and a fan will remark, 'We won!' Oh, *you* won? You all did it, did you? It wasn't the athletes with painstaking training and commitment above all else? It was you shouting aggressive praise bordering on abuse at a television. Just being a fan of something, that means you helped it happen? Okay then! Well in that case I am very excited to announce that in 2007, along with my teammate Tilda Swinton, I won the Academy Award for Best Actress in a Supporting Role for our stellar work in Tony Gilroy's wonderful film *Michael Clayton*. It was a career best for the two of us and I would appreciate it if you could please respect my privacy at this exciting time.

I think I like silly sports. Sports where the players don't look like athletes. Golf, for example. Most elite-level golfers look like the quiet guy your aunty just started dating later in life who keeps calling you buddy. There are certain sports that I think I would enjoy the lifestyle of if I put in the effort. Motorsports like the F1 are up there. I couldn't give a shit about the actual races, of course, but the drivers are handsome and the clientele seem to be doing a lot of gin-drinking and linen-wearing. I can do that. Tennis. For years Kyran has been trying to get me into playing tennis. Or even go to watch it with him. He'll never succeed, and I've not been able to explain to him why, for some reason, the idea of it just leaves a bad taste in my mouth. I'm not talking in metaphors.

I take you back to early 2009. Barack Obama had just become president, there was talk of a new app called Grindr and we were still a few months away from the planet-shifting effects of Kanye interrupting Taylor Swift. They were simpler, almost cocoon-like times of ease and bliss. It was the beginning of my second year working at a burger shop in my hometown, a job I truly loved. You got a free burger for every six hours you worked and there were so many people working there no one really noticed if you wandered off and stood in the cool room for up to twenty-five minutes with your hand placed on a box of meat so if anyone came looking for you, you could say you were just getting more patties for the grill. Needless to say I was really, really bad at it but I've never let something like that get in my way. It was the type of establishment where extreme efforts are made to encourage you to think an incredibly unhealthy thing you're eating is actually not bad for you at all because we'd put a wafer-thin sliver of avocado on it and given it a fun name like Greener Pastures. When the owners, a cool couple in their early forties, were there the collection of idle teenagers they called their staff were all on our best behaviour. Making sharp and decisive movements to get the food out on time. Laser focused on delivering what the customers might like. As soon as the coast was clear, however, we got back to our real work. Well, research, really: trying to see what would happen if you put unsanctioned foods in the deep-fryer. We considered ourselves a sort of radical branch of the CSIRO, testing the limits of what boiling hot oil could do. A word of warning: if ever, and I mean *ever*, a fast-food place claims their chips are vegetarian, they aren't. A hugely hungover eighteen-year-old has definitely chucked a whole barnyard of meats in there out of pure curiosity.

It was around 10 pm on a Saturday night and at the end of my shift I was furious to realise I'd forgotten to bring a change of clothes. This meant I would have to spend the evening reeking of animal fats. I usually wouldn't care too much because growing up as a fat kid, in a weird way I find that smell quite comforting. Similar to the feeling I experienced recently when I heard my friend's voice on a TV show in the background of an amateur porn I was watching. It's a little triggering and then intimately quite nice. The beef odour on this occasion would be inconvenient because I had a plan that night to go out and make some new friends at a party where I didn't know anyone. The past few months had been a vaguely complicated stretch of time for me. My whole vibe had ever so slightly commenced a shift for a few reasons. I was with finished with high school, a whole troupe of my friends had moved away to go to uni, I'd shed quite a bit of weight, started wearing my hair differently and was becoming quite the connoisseur of cheap, premixed, very alcoholic energy drinks. All these elements combined gave me the high level of wild-eyed confidence only quite a bit of low self-esteem can produce. I was bored of being boring. I was giving fervent consent to the universe.

My cab turned down the quiet suburban street and came to a stop out the front of a wide, two-storey brick house with the type of strange ornate features suburban people whack on their homes so you know they have money. I remember thinking I bet they have French doors on their fridge and more than one Foxtel box in the house. It was a place for someone who goes to Bali every year as a family and when talking about it might say something vague and terrible like, 'They're just a *beau*tiful people over there.' This was the house of a friend of a friend of a friend of a friend repeated, hosting the genre of party you went to when you were nineteen for a few hours and then quietly left after you had broken something precious like an urn, or thrown up somewhere terrible like an urn.

For more than an hour since the end of my shift I'd been texting a kind of friend who was meant to be coming with me, but I wasn't getting a reply from her. She was a bit of a social liability dirtbag and the two of us barely knew each other, but we'd gone to school together and were making an effort to become closer since almost all our friends had fled town. We'd both become so lonely we'd moved up the ranks of one another's friendship rosters. Not unlike when Osama bin Laden and his pals were killed, suddenly there was a whole new slew of faces on the World's Most Wanted list. Her potential no-show meant I was alone. Fuck. The idea of having to interact with people I didn't know at all was and is still haunting to me. I'll never understand people who can just talk to someone they don't know. I don't want to talk to the people I *do* know (I haven't answered my phone in over a decade). I wish adults could be like eight-year-olds and just walk up to someone and say out loud 'Will you be my friend?' without the hassle of having to do shitloads of MDMA first.

After waiting out the front for almost twenty minutes and watching several other guests arrive, I downed a Cruiser, tailgated some others and found myself inside. It was now after 11 pm and in full swing. Teenagers littered the house in little clumps surrounding their stashes of booze as if they were handbag dancing around goon sacks. I needed to find a clump as soon as possible. In a corner I made some final, unsuccessful attempts to make contact with my date when I looked up and found myself making eye contact with someone. A very particular kind of eye contact. The 'you're the other gay at this party' eye contact. Across the room stood a guy around my age alongside a clearly already very drunk girl wearing cat ears. Still not completely sure if he had been looking at me, I glanced behind myself to see if there was someone else there, only to find a marble side table with a single bowl of shells on it. As I looked back, he beckoned me over so I focused all my energy drink buzz into a ball of nerve and wandered across. As soon as I arrived it became clear he had come with his very own social liability dirtbag. I had been beaconed over as a possible saviour. As a conversation sparked up, she alternated at whiplash pace between looking at her phone, complaining she was bored and using the phrase 'my gays' in as many sentences as possible. It got to the point where me and this guy were talking across her the way a parent might do at a cafe as their toddler tries to interject while pawing at their face and neck for attention. We will call my new friend Christopher, I suppose. Not to protect his identity, I just genuinely can't remember his name. And it seems like most gay men in hometowns are named Christopher. Christopher or Dylan. We volleyed conversation back and forth as we laughed and tried to work out if we knew each other or had mutual friends. Eventually the Mother of Gays became so bored she up and left. When I asked Christopher what her vibe was, he replied, 'Oh, she's a real cunt but this is a great house for parties.' I couldn't tell if he was a nightmare or the best person I'd ever met. Exactly my type. For another hour or so we chatted, said some horrific things about people just out of earshot, and I think I may have broken a mug, so it was decided we'd go for a walk. Sure, why not. Having both finished the drinks we'd brought we embarked on a little quest and upstairs in one of the spare rooms we found and stole a box of Fruity Lexia someone had stashed, then we were on our way.

With the Australian summer in its final death throes, the night was warm, and the goon was warmer. We walked and silently passed the sack between us. After a while we stopped, he initiated a kiss and we dry humped a bit against a bus shelter. It's moments like this I see why people become hardcore hometown burnouts. Why try and do anything with your life or even leave the country when you can just coast and aggressively rub boners that are all cooped up in your skinny jeans on the street at 2 am? Christopher looked up and as he gestured across the street said, 'Let's go in there.' I knew that place, it was the Broadmeadow outdoor tennis courts. I used to go there for school sport. The rusty fence was an easy climb. We found ourselves a spot and got back to it. We're standing up in this kind of hut thing making out. Kissing has never done it for me, frankly. I actually find if quite funny and have trouble doing it for very long before I get bored. Someone told me not too long ago that she and her husband regularly still have make-out sessions that lead to nothing past some over-the-jeans action. Having been together for more than a decade they are getting down to it like teenagers on the couch watching a Blockbuster weekly movie deal. And yes, of course, intimacy means different things to everyone and everything and blah blah blah but personally, if we are kissing for more than four minutes I better at least be seeing a penis.

So, on a pitch-black tennis court in suburban Newcastle, I unbuckled his jeans and I went downstairs because I was raised to be nice to new friends. And I was down there, and without divulging too many of the gory details, everything was going great. But then out of nowhere, it wasn't. The mixture of the energy drinks, the goon, the movement – I gagged a bit. Which was uncommon for me at this point in my life; usually you could open an umbrella in there. But I continued. *It's fine,* I thought. I gagged again. *It's fine. I'm fine.* Then like Icarus – or Dickarus – I flew too close to the sun. It was too late. A waterfall of fermented fruit poured over his lap. A Niagara Falls of cheap liquor and shame. He gasped as if . . . well, as if someone just vomited on him mid-fellatio.

I gotta say, it was pretty damn quiet for a bit there. I offered my work apron out of my backpack as a cleaning option. He obliged and we made our way over the fence with our eyes looking anywhere but each other. We waved goodbye and walked in opposite directions. I never saw him again, which is quite the feat in Newcastle. I've never told anyone but always wonder who he told and if it ever got its way down the friends of friends of friends Silk Road.

I caught up with a schoolfriend not long ago. The guy who was meant to come to that party with me, actually. We were reminiscing about school sport and in particular how bad we were at tennis. 'God we sucked,' he said.

THE OLD GUARD

While procrastinating from a quite important deadline, I often find myself doing what I always do when something really, really needs to get done: noodling around the internet, letting my finely tuned algorithms take me where I need to go for the highest amounts of dopamine and avoidance as possible. YouTube, Instagram, even in its death throes sometimes Twitter can still give me what I need. I have a system, for this is not just your average procrastination. I've spent almost two decades refining my technique to a fine art. I could write an entire book about it if I could find the time. The key is to let yourself be taken by the dilly-dallying for about twenty minutes, telling yourself you'll get back to your more pressing task straight afterwards. When twenty minutes is up, look at your task. Really look at it. Feel as stressed and as guilty as possible about how you haven't been working on it. Really marinate in those feelings. Stare at your task, making your eyes as wide as possible to cram your optic nerve with the sheer breadth and depth of what you should actually be doing. Think about all the time you haven't spent on it. After about forty-five minutes of this intense activity, you'll be majorly exhausted and ready for another twenty-minute break. Hey, you've earned it. Give it a try, why don't you, and let me know how it goes. I can't guarantee I'll reply because I have quite a few emails backed up, for some reason.

Some days I cast myself adrift in Wikipedia. Not too long ago I bargained with myself that if I am going to wade into the calm, warm waters of unaccountability, I may as well learn something along the way. Link to link to link to link. Click, click, click, click. I hop from one page to the next, hoovering up useless facts and filling what precious last bits of ram I have left in my brain. Aimlessly noodling around the internet is my happy place and it's become a real problem. Nothing to worry myself about, though. That's future Rhys's problem. That guy has a lot on their plate. Me? Current Rhys? Easy breezy. Sure, I have trouble remembering important dates and responsibilities such as birthdays or how to give CPR, but did you know the original voice cast of *Captain Planet* included Whoopi Goldberg, Martin Sheen, Jeff Goldblum and, in my opinion, a career best from Meg Ryan? Did you know the guy at the start of the movie *Hook* who gets put into a box is Glenn Close in drag? And did you know I have no idea how tax works? One day I'd clicked and clicked until finally I was resting my eyes on a page about, believe it or not, llamas. A bonkers creature the longer you look at it. It's nature's answer to the question, 'What if a sheep and a giraffe had a baby and it was furious at you to the point of spitting?' More specifically, I was reading about guard llamas. No, I'm not talking about a new indie band out of Perth. I mean llamas who guard property or livestock. I had never heard about them, so imagine my surprise and delight when I learned that in some countries they use these lanky creatures to watch over livestock on farms. 'What do you mean?' I literally mumbled out loud to myself. How does something like this happen? One of the wildest parts I found out as I read on was that you don't really have to train them up at all. If you put a llama among a flock of lambs, it will instinctively just start watching them and keep the herd safe from harm. By this point I had entirely thrown away the idea of ever finishing the task that was due and was now full pelt down a YouTube chasm watching these guys in action. I highly recommend it. Foxes, coyotes and even some wolves. Each time the predator approaches the vulnerable lambs, the llama charges forward without an iota of hesitation. Sometimes they protect by sheer force and sometimes you can see in the footage the fox wander over, then notice what must look like a gargantuan mutant sheep on stilts and just get the fuck out of there. Llamas: nature's secret service.

It must be nice, to have that type of trust put in you. To have some internal instinct that just switches on to save the day, day after day. An innate want to help others and keep them safe. I know plenty of people who possess this: my partner, my family, my agents. I decidedly do not hold this inborn tendency. Your ol' pal Rhyso is a real sheep in this metaphor. I'm probably not even a good sheep, because at least sheep are followers. I can't even follow very well. I think I just get unknowingly lightly nudged into place by a small group of dedicated individuals. A full herd of llamas watching over this singular, little dumb-dumb lamb.

As we stretch this already quite thin analogy even closer to breaking point, I put it to you that in your life, you can boil anyone down to two camps. The llamas and the sheep. It's a spectrum, of course, but each and every meaningful relationship, romantic or otherwise, requires at least one of each to exist. The llamas are the pragmatists to keep things moving along, while the sheep mostly let the world trickle over them as they try their hardest not to make too much of a fuss. It's basically the people who complain at restaurants when an order is wrong and the people who stand behind that person mouthing the word 'sorry' to the waitstaff.

It's not a one and done situation, this llama business. You can easily have several of them working concurrently in the one gene pool, but there will always be one to rule them all – a leader of leaders; a sort of grand high llama. It could be anyone and although not strictly gender based, we can probably agree it's almost always a woman. More often than not, it's a woman letting a man believe he is in fact the llama. He isn't. He's just a big sheep trying to tell everyone what to do while she's nodding and quietly trafficking the herd around. In my family tree, there is no doubt who ours is. When I was about five, my parents, my sister and I, through circumstances that are none of our business, had to move in with my grandmother, Nancy. A few years earlier she had been widowed far too soon in life after my grandfather Owen, the undisputed and much-loved patriarch of our clan, had passed away. She gladly took us in to her big empty house and did whatever she had to do to help us get our shit together.

Throughout the next little while my parents worked an absolute fucktonne so Granny and I spent a lot of time with each other. Wherever she went, I went. During weekdays this involved a lot of visiting. Old people bloody love to visit each other. They're utterly obsessed with a morning tea and a catch-up. It's as if they want to service the meaningful relationships in their lives. I find it all very peculiar. I suppose it's what you had to do to fill the time before there was the option to sit on the corner of your bed for several hours, scrolling alternating social media apps before settling into a bit of a panic attack in the afternoon.

We'd visit in the morning but every day we'd be sure to get back home to catch our soaps, *Days of our Lives* and *The Young and the Restless*. But never, ever *The Bold and the Beautiful*. According to Nancy, that show is utter trash for people with nothing to do in the afternoons. Our shows were just a treat in between tasks as we ate lunch. The two of us, with our sixty-year age gap, eating corned beef sandwiches, would sit together in her frozen-in-time loungeroom and discuss the episodes. There was so much going on! What would be the exciting ramifications now Marlene has been possessed by the devil himself? Will this affect Stefano's important cocktail party? How do they make their hair so big? Then Granny would get back to her errands, chores and teaching me how to sew. Sometimes I'm not sure if I'm gay or perhaps I'm just deeply emulating my hero, a woman born in the late 1930s.

After a couple years we moved out, and by this point I was at school. I hated school so much and would often, and I mean often, fake being sick so I didn't have to go. She'd never admit it, but having not been a huge fan of school herself, I'm almost certain she was happy to play along. I recall being so devastated to not have so much time with Granny. My sister is much older than me so she was out having fun. Luckily on Fridays, Granny would pick me up at school and I would stay at her place. At the time I thought of this as a treat for me, but now I think about it, it was most definitely so Mum and Dad could have some well-deserved time to themselves. Plus I had to know what was happening on our shows now school was getting in the way. Friday nights meant two things with Granny: we'd watch a movie and she would cook one of my absolute favourites, fried rice that was so goddamned delicious but can only be described as deeply, deeply Caucasian in its execution and taste. Granny, like many women of her generation, had never gotten over the advancements in modern kitchen technology. Anyone born after the late 1970s might take something as simple as the microwave oven for granted, whereas these ladies are passionate about magnetrons and the way they make the molecules of food vibrate to the point of frictional heat. She's the only person I've ever seen microwave bacon before popping it into the rice.

I'm biased, but whenever the phrase 'They are just of their time' is used to explain someone's problematic views, I think of Granny. Because of just how irrelevant the sentiment is to her. I never had to come out to her. When I was about seventeen I was invited to go on a float at the Sydney Mardi Gras. The news reached Granny and when I saw her next she asked if I was 'Ready for the big day?' A cousin of mine recently changed their name and pronouns and there is Granny, in her late eighties trying her best not to deadname. She's so easily grasped that times change and that's usually a good thing. I think if you're fortunate enough to have a good grandparent, it's safe to say we're getting the best of them. We're lucky as grandchildren. For as long as I can remember, Nancy has had a magnet on her fridge that reads, 'If I had known grandchildren were so much fun, I would have had them first.' It's good stuff. As a child I took this as a beacon of hope to my generation of cousins. It let us know this lady was on our side. Of course as an adult I can also now see she's absolutely fucking roasting our parents for everything they must have put her through when they were young. It must have been strange for our parents to see the shift a grandparent like her makes. Mum sometimes remarks on the stunning transition Nancy has gone through since she was little. Having been a working mother of four in the fifties and sixties, she's apparently far softer than the 1960s working mother they had experienced. The way older siblings of the family talk it's as if she's been gentrified like a tough suburb. When I call Granny, which is not at all often enough, I ask her what she's been up to, and she tells me how she's been rewatching *Game Of Thrones*, noting that Jason Momoa is 'a good sort'. She's read more books than anyone I know. When I visit her, which is not nearly enough, sometimes I will read the back cover blurb of that day's tome and notice it is some deeply horny tale set during a war somewhere exotic. If you tease her about it she'll arc right up and make you very aware: 'At least it's not Danielle Steele! At least it has a story!' This flabbergasts my mother like you wouldn't believe. Mum can often be heard remarking on how this same woman, sixty years ago, was so coy she couldn't even muster up the courage to say the word 'breast' in front of the butcher. 'Years of having to eat bloody drumsticks,' she says, 'and now her favourite shows are basically hardcore porn!'

At eighty-nine, Granny is still sharp and kicking but undeniably her world is, by her own design, getting smaller. These days she seems happier at family gatherings in a role closer to a spectator and fact checker. Piping up from time to time to correct a story being exaggerated by one of her kids. 'Oh, it wasn't that bad,' she'll assert. Then if one of them pulls her up on some sort of inaccuracy, she'll lovingly snap back with one of her all-time classic lines, 'Don't ruin a good story with the truth.' When a vaguely annoying distant relative arrived at a function a while back, I watched Granny turn her hearing aid down. When this person tried talking to her, she just pointed at her ears and shrugged as if she was powerless to it. I think I'm most blown away by how she keeps up with her duty as a grandparent and now great-grandparent with her seemingly genuine interest in all our lives. Every Christmas and birthday, both Kyran and I, along with all my cousins and their partners, get a card with $50 each in it. Every time she writes how proud she is about some specific thing in our lives and always finishes with, 'I love you both. Thank you for loving me.' Even in her advanced years and as we begin to grow our own families, she's keeping a watchful eye on all of us. Her herd.

WILDLY BASIC AND DISRESPECTFULLY CAUCASIAN FRIED RICE

– SERVES: FOUR–SIX –

– PREPARATION TIME: TWENTY MINUTES –

– COOKING TIME: TWENTY–TWENTY-FIVE MINUTES –

– INGREDIENTS –

12 rashers streaky bacon, chopped into 2 cm squares

2 tbsp vegetable oil

1 small onion, peeled and finely diced

2 cloves garlic, peeled and minced

1 carrot, peeled and finely diced

2 eggs, lightly beaten

½ cup frozen peas

2 cups cooked long-grain rice (preferably chilled or day-old rice)

3 tbsp soy sauce

2 tbsp sesame oil

1 tbsp oyster sauce

2 spring onions, sliced

salt and pepper (optional)

– METHOD –

- Place some paper towel on a microwave-safe plate then shovel half the bacon on there and spread it out evenly. Microwave for around 4 minutes until it's crispy. Repeat the process with the other half of the bacon. This is going to feel counter-productive and you're going to wonder why you don't just fry it in a pan. Your intuition is correct.

- Heat a large frying pan or wok (oh lah-di-dah) over some medium–high heat and add the vegetable oil. Swirl it around to coat the bottom of the pan evenly.

- Add the diced onion and sauté for 2–3 minutes until it becomes translucent and slightly golden. Stir but make sure to forget a couple times so it's slightly burnt.

- Add the minced garlic and bacon to the pan and cook for another 30 seconds until fragrant. Yes, again, I agree the bacon could have gone in earlier.

- Toss in the finely diced carrot and cook for about 2 minutes until it begins to soften. You should be pretty constantly moving everything around so it cooks evenly. Now push the vegetables to one side of the frying pan and pour the beaten eggs into the empty space. Let the eggs cook undisturbed for a few seconds until they start to set.

- Break up the partially cooked eggs with a spatula and scramble them. Allow the eggs to cook completely until no liquid remains.

- Add the frozen peas and stir everything together. Cook for another 1–2 minutes until the peas are heated through.

- Increase the heat to high and add the rice. Get to work with a wooden spoon to break up any clumps. You're aiming for the vegetables, eggs and rice to be evenly mixed together.

- Drizzle soy sauce, oyster sauce and sesame oil over the rice. Remember, this is basically the only thing giving this cursed dish any flavour whatsoever. Toss everything together until the sauces are well incorporated and the rice is evenly coated.

- Continue stir-frying the rice for another 3–4 minutes, allowing it to heat through and develop some crispy edges. Adjust the seasoning with salt and pepper according to your taste, though bear in mind that soy sauce is basically liquid salt, so you might want to go easy.

- Finally, camply sprinkle spring onions over the fried rice and give it a final toss. Serve into a single bowl and show this to no one. This is your secret. Display the leftovers in your fridge for several days by which time you have forgotten about it and it's transformed into poison.

BODY OF WORK

Do you ever find yourself browsing your local pharmacy? One of those big ones you only see outside city centres? An enormous suburban barn of discounted painkillers, off-brand make-up and perfumes endorsed by long-forgotten reality stars. Aisle upon aisle where everything is somehow permanently on sale and although there seem to be countless members of staff tidying the shelves at all times, the shop itself always looks well and truly war-torn. I like these places. I like them because there is always something going on inside. A bit of spicy local action to observe. There might be a pensioner being furiously passive-aggressive to the checkout attendant for the long wait. Maybe you glimpse a nineteen-year-old fuckboi taking his time to very openly and performatively check out the protein powders. Perhaps it's simply a toddler scream-crying at the hip of its mother while she stares dead eyed into the middle distance of the contraceptive aisle, her mind wandering to a bygone era of personal space, long lie-ins and brunch. A trip to the mega pharmacy affords us all a stark reminder that no matter how shit you think your day is going, someone is having a worse time of it.

Once a month I venture into my neighbourhood pharmacy to do what I call my 'embarrassing shop', when I walk around a public space with a shopping basket overflowing with some of the more distressing items available on the market. I like these products. I'll buy almost anything that makes me an impossible guarantee. The sorts of things I would describe as quick fixes. I am, unashamedly, incredibly vain, but unfortunately simultaneously very lazy. So I need the merchandise that will promise results for as little effort as possible. There's the painful wax I use to rip out the small shrub of nose hair I've started growing. That exact same shade of hair dye I've been using for over fifteen years. The medicated body wash that helps manage a stress rash that appears on my back and tummy in the warmer months. A parade of various lotions, potions and salves that help the parts of my body that are too dry get wetter and the bits that are too wet get dryer. Not to mention several remedies that, depending on how the month has been, will help me either start or stop shitting. Also sometimes lube. This whole retail process is very important to me as it's a monthly reminder that while, yes, life as a concept is miraculous and awe-inspiring, the act of actually being alive is in fact quite embarrassing and basically pretty fucking disgusting.

Kyran, on the other hand, is one of those maddening people who somehow just wakes up looking ready for the day. He washes his face with regular soap, has had maybe six pimples during the course of our entire relationship, and the man's complexion is effortlessly smooth, apart from a few shallow laugh lines, indicating he feels joy. I was absolutely thrilled a few years ago when his thick head of hair began prematurely greying. *Yes!* I thought, *People will know he's ageing now!* But devastatingly it's developed into a kind of David Byrne/ Steve Martin/Mr Sheffield vibe so is categorically more of an asset at this point. Another bitter disappointment. In the one drawer of our bathroom dedicated to Kyran's beauty regime sits a singular comb, for sale, never used.

I'm thirty-three. Which of course is not old. Not old at all, really. But it certainly feels old enough. Not old enough for anything specifically, just old enough. I reckon I'd be happy to stop this absurd ageing process right here, to be honest. The rot has begun. I first felt the crest of the ageing bell curve about four years ago. Back then I was just twenty-nine and very, very young. Friends who were much, much older – some as mature as thirty-four – would warn me of the risks associated with turning thirty. As it was explained to me, a teeny-tiny-twenties baby, the big three-o signalled new perspectives. Some were at the smaller end of the spectrum: maybe a change in diet; less drinking; a greater focus on spending time with loved ones; perhaps even a new and self-improving hobby. The common denominator was maintenance. As if the new decade revealed life as a cosmic garden, and these older friends were lovingly tending to it. Planting a few fresh saplings for a more enriching future and taking a moment to smell the roses. Sounds lovely. On the other, heavier side of the scales were the people who plummeted into their thirties and hit the deck with a thud. Instead of slight, focused alterations, they'd gone with something closer to a complete life explosion. Partners were left. Jobs were quit. The garden was not just entirely bulldozed, but the soil was then salted and the landscaping staff forced to dig their own shallow graves before they were shot, execution style, and the whole thing concreted over.

Okay, maybe the gardening metaphor has run away from me, but you get what I mean. Some big changes were made. As I've grown older, I've started to notice these moments of so-called clarity happening around me. A whole bunch of mates in my orbit have spent loads of time picking up entire chunks of their lives and asking themselves if it sparks joy. And I find it all terribly discombobulating. Such behaviour can come across as a cry for help, but as a spectator there are not always clear indicators to tell when someone is doing it for the right or wrong reason. The question is when, if ever, should you interfere? Are they in trouble or are they fine? Are they flourishing or hurtling off a cliff? Who knows? After all, both situations look identical to the innocent though concerned bystander. I'm sure you know the feeling. Suddenly there is no small talk with these people – it's all big chats about big things and big plans. And to be honest, who am I to say they're wrong? Sure, their life might seem a little wild and sketchy, but why should I hold them back? Some of the most successful businesses on Etsy are the result of a several full-blown manic episodes. Sometimes you just must make a call, though. In one particularly dramatic instance, a pal of mine left her long-term partner and considered moving into one of those tiny homes you see in documentaries late at night on free-to-air digital channels. At that point I had to step in. A real friend doesn't let another human being use a compost toilet.

Given how vain I am, it's come as a surprise that I don't mind the fact I'm starting to look a little older. My face is beginning to betray that I have at times felt joy. There are upsides (the fact I no longer have to take ID to bottle shops and bars must be saving me hours of time a year). Sure, I hit up the pharmacy every few months to stock up on my favourite lightly corrosive retinoids to use on my face, but nothing drastic – just a little bit of skin trauma to bully it into making more collagen. What a thrill to be at a point in my life where I'm spooking my biggest organ.

However, the likes of injectables don't interest me so much. My flesh-deep anxieties live elsewhere. As I get ever so slightly older, those all-too-familiar clichés start to make more and more sense. 'Youth is wasted on the young,' for example. I know it sounds insane to say that at thirty-three, but recently I was spring-cleaning my phone and came across a picture of myself from when I was about nineteen. I'm standing in a park, hungover, staring down the barrel of the camera with a sultry smile, appearing profoundly tired. I look hot. I'm sorry, but it has to be said. I am strikingly beautiful in this picture. Chiselled and sparkling. At the very height of my twinkdom powers. To look at me you'd think, *This babe must be cleaning up out there.* Their pelvic bone must be near mush by now. I hope they're staying hydrated. It was strange for me to view this image now because I can't unsee, even through the smile, how tremendously unhappy I was back then. So wildly convinced that not only was I not attractive, I was hideous. What I can see now in that photo is a person standing on the edge of a cliff, seconds away from falling into quite a nasty abyss that they will stay in for several years.

I have an eating disorder. It took me a long time, contending with a whole bunch of emotional and mental gymnastics, plus some good ol' fashioned delusion, to put words to it, but I have one. Not had. Have. I am, thank fuck, in recovery, and have been for years.

But unfortunately, although I'm no longer practising, culturally, I am body dysmorphic. To go too much into the gory, physical details would not be pleasant or helpful so I won't bother with any of that. No one wants this to devolve into trauma porn fan fiction. But, base level facts: from about the age of nineteen through to twenty-four, I went to some atrocious lengths to shrink myself down to the size and shape you'd sooner expect to see on a long-since-dead corpse flopped onto the autopsy table in a Scandi crime-drama about a serial killer who's hoarding all their victims' body fat. (If any network execs are reading, my working title is *The Weight Watcher Murders.*)

It's difficult to explain how you get there. A fusion of things, I suppose. A heaped pile of tiny moments that equate to anorexia by a thousand cuts. My first memory of stacking some Shame Coal into the Sad Furnace is probably when I was a chubby little kid and my uncle was married to a horrible, vapid woman who whenever she saw me would point at my little prepubescent pot belly and ask me when the baby was due. That's definitely in the mix. Then, when I naturally lost weight in my late teens, the sudden attention I received from boys was of course just the right amount of toxic reinforcement I needed to stoke the fires of self-disgust. And finally, when I'd moved to Sydney and flung myself into the noxious twinky gay bar scene, the steady diet of uppers, double vodka Red Bulls, cigarettes and sex acts on pretty boys who liked me because I was thin probably didn't help either. At least I was getting some protein.

I've begun to consider my eating disorder as something like having a substance abuse problem. When you're well, it's a little thing that's always in the back of your brain to keep an eye on. But when you're unwell, you find yourself in a constant state of telling yourself you have it under control. You're definitely going to stop. Very soon. Just a couple more kilos. Just a tiny bit smaller. I just want to be smaller. When I first started, I instantly became a master at rationalising completely, indisputably irrational behaviour. Lying became my friend. 'Oh no, I actually ate before I came, so I'm fine. But you guys eat!' I developed specialised skills to move around and hide food on a plate, like some grim, carbs-based close-up magician. I remember physically cringing when I'd go back to my hometown and someone in my family would say I was 'looking healthy'. Ergh. To someone in that situation, looking healthy means you simply aren't working hard enough. Smaller. I just wanted to be smaller. By twenty-three years old I was five foot ten and sitting at about 58 kilos. I looked awful. Today, it's so utterly bizarre to try and imagine being in a place where the way I was treating myself and my body made no fucking sense at all. It's bonkers and to be honest, really, really embarrassing. I'm embarrassed by my complete lack of self-worth.

I'm lucky, because I was able to stop before it was too late. Could I have finished up a little earlier had I listened to and accepted the concern being offered around me? Oh, absolutely. Without a doubt. Kyran was the linchpin. We'd begun dating and then quite quickly moved in together. It was suddenly much more difficult to play out my nasty business of tricks and misdirects. He wasn't just someone I was partying with at bars, or a family member that saw me every few weeks. He had the full picture. For the first time, I had a witness. After a few months he'd started to lightly confront me about it until I finally stopped blowing it off as none of his business and we talked about it. Then talked some more. Still never calling it what it was. 'My eating thing', I labelled it. Over time I spoke more and more openly. Far too soon I foolishly did what I always do when I don't know how to deal with something not remotely funny: I wrote some wildly ill-informed stand-up about it and pretended this meant I'd sorted it. I figured if I was using it, it didn't have a hold on me anymore. I was even featured in a segment about male eating disorders on a topical investigative news show, *The Feed*. The irony of talking about it on a show called *The Feed* was not lost on me, but no one found it funny when I kept bringing it up on air. You can find it still on YouTube, and I gotta say, for me, it's a hard watch. To my eyes today I am so clearly still in it. Right in the centre of the illness. It's like watching a reporter proudly announce the winning of a war as they dodge gunfire and take shelter in the rubble of a demolished house. There was quite a bit more work to do.

Thankfully, thirty didn't hit me too hard. I didn't explode my life because I kind of already had. I'm glad I'm ageing. If anything, I yearn to be positively ancient. To get to that point where your bathroom drawers aren't crammed with products and you aren't chasing anything anymore. To go around with a vague sense that you're doing okay. It's a feeling that could be confused with born-again Christianity and those types of people who are at peace with themselves and their bodies. At the risk of sounding so severely sincere, I am so wildly glad that I am getting older because it means I am still alive and thank fuck, looking healthy.

A WILDLY BASIC YET DEEPLY COMFORTING FRIED CHICKEN SANDWICH

Eat. For fuck's sake, eat.

– SERVES: FOUR. OR I DON'T KNOW, ALSO JUST ONE. MAYBE IT'S BEEN A BIG DAY. YOU DO YOU –

– PREPARATION TIME: CLOSE TO AN HOUR IF YOU'RE BEING LEISURELY, PLUS OVERNIGHT MARINATING –

– COOKING TIME: ABOUT TWENTY MINUTES –

– INGREDIENTS –

Marinade

1 cup buttermilk
½ cup pickle juice
1 tbsp hot sauce of your choice (I use Frank's)
4 chicken thigh fillets, skin off
1 cup plain flour
1 tsp paprika
1 tsp garlic powder
1 tsp salt
½ tsp black pepper
vegetable oil, for frying

Slaw

2 cups shredded cabbage (green or red)

1 carrot, peeled and grated

¼ cup mayonnaise

1 tbsp apple cider vinegar

1 tsp sugar

salt and pepper, to taste

Mayo, baby!

1 cup mayonnaise

2 tbsp finely chopped parsley

1 tbsp finely chopped dill

1 tbsp finely chopped chives

1 garlic clove, peeled and finely grated

2 tbsp fresh lemon juice

½ tsp celery seeds

½ tsp freshly ground black pepper

For the assembly

4 burger buns of your choice

(I prefer a seeded hamburger bun – brioche is dead to me)

2 tbsp melted butter

8 thick coins of dill pickle

– METHOD –

- Combine the buttermilk, pickle juice and hot sauce in a bowl then add the chicken and move it all around so the bird is completely coated in its sweet death brine. Cover the bowl and let the chicken marinate in the refrigerator for at least 1 hour, but overnight is waaaaaay better.

For the slaw

- Toss the slaw ingredients together in a large bowl. Adjust seasoning to taste. Cover and refrigerate until ready to assemble the sandwiches.

For the mayo

- Mix it all up and, you guessed it, refrigerate until ready to assemble the sandwiches. The flavours need to spend a little time together to have a conversation so you can do this a few hours/the night before you plan to eat your feast of dead chicken between carbs.

Fry the chicken

- In a shallow dish, combine flour, paprika, garlic powder, salt and pepper. Add about a tablespoon or two of the buttermilk marinade to the flour mixture and move it around a little with your fingers to get a few shaggy bits coming together. This is going to help get some crispy morsels going on the meat while it's frying.

- Remove the chicken from the buttermilk, allowing any excess to drip off. Dredge the chicken in the seasoned flour mixture, pressing it onto both sides to coat evenly.

- Heat the oil in a deep fryer to 175°C, or fill a heavy pot or wok with about 5–7 cm of vegetable oil and use a kitchen thermometer to check it heats to 175°C. Carefully place the coated chicken breasts into the hot oil and fry for about 6–8 minutes per side or until golden brown and cooked through. (You can use a meat thermometer to check the internal temperature is 75°C). Transfer the fried chicken to a paper towel-lined plate to drain any excess oil.

Assemble the sandwiches

- Slice the burger buns in half, brush a small amount of melted butter onto the cut sides and lightly toast in a cast iron frying pan over a medium heat until brown. Remove and spread spicy mayonnaise on the bottom half of each bun. Place a fried chicken breast on top. Top the chicken with a generous amount of slaw, adding a couple of pickle slices atop the slaw if you like. You could whack a couple of dashes of hot sauce in there, too.

- Eat it openly and without deep-seated shame.

A WILDLY BASIC YET DEEPLY COMFORTING SPICED APPLE TARTE TATIN

Keep eating.

– SERVES: ONE–SIX –

– PREPARATION TIME: FIFTEEN MINUTES –

– COOKING TIME: AN HOUR –

– INGREDIENTS –

6–8 apples (a mixture of Granny Smith and golden delicious works well)
1 cup granulated sugar
125 g unsalted butter
1 tsp vanilla extract
1 tsp ground cinnamon
¼ tsp ground nutmeg
¼ tsp ground cloves
1 sheet puff pastry, thawed
schmancy vanilla ice cream, to serve

– METHOD –

- Preheat your oven to 190°C fan-forced (210°C conventional).

- Peel, core, and slice the apples into quarter wedges. Set them aside. Don't bother worrying if they are going to brown. No one will notice once they are baked. Calm down.

- Heat the sugar in a 22 cm oven-safe frying pan over a low heat, stirring until it melts and turns into a toffee-like sauce. It's toffee-like because it is in fact toffee now. Be careful not to burn it. Once it's melted, take it off the heat and stir in the butter with a wooden spoon. It's going to seem angry at you about this. Keep stirring and she'll settle down. There, you have some caramel now.

- Add the vanilla extract, cinnamon, nutmeg and cloves. Stir well to combine and let the caramel cool for a minute or two in the frying pan.

- Arrange the apple slices in a spiral pattern on top of the spiced caramel. You can pack them tightly as they will experience some, ahem, shrinkage. Nothing to be embarrassed about.

- Return the pan to the stove over a medium heat and cook the apples for about 10 minutes without turning until they soften slightly and there's some browning on the undercarriage (lol).

- While the apples are cooking, roll out the puff pastry sheet on a lightly floured surface until it is large enough to cover the frying pan.

- Carefully place the puff pastry over the cooked apples, tucking in the edges around them, trimming off any excess.

- Using a fork, prick the surface of the puff pastry to allow steam to escape during baking.

- Place the pan in the preheated oven and bake for 25–30 minutes, or until the pastry has risen, is golden brown and crispy.

- Remove from the oven and allow to cool for a few minutes.

- Place a serving plate upside down over the frying pan and carefully flip it over to release the tarte tatin onto the plate. Be careful as the caramel sauce will be as hot as the centre of the earth.

- It's tarte tatin! Serve with vanilla ice cream.

HOW TO WRITE YOUR FIRST BOOK: PART VI

Done. It's finally fucking done.

You did it. You're a published author now. An esteemed member of a community of people famous for their self-belief, staggering wealth and high levels of creative output.

Is it late? Oh yes, quite late. Well and truly beyond the decided delivery date, strictly managed by your publisher. Now would be a good time to brush up on your quantum physics to help explain to your editor that time, and in fact the contracted word count, is just a concept.

Now begins the editing process. Ooft. As you venture down the rabbit warren of cuts, feedback and questions about the choices you've made, your instinct is going to hate everything you've done so far. Each and every word is going to feel clunky, laboured, inept, unwieldy, heavy and wrong. You may even think you perhaps use too many synonyms sometimes. No. Ignore that voice. Lean into the lukewarm pool of delusion. Start prematurely asking questions about book launches and panel events. Pitch ideas about swag bags and edible party favours. Openly bring up that when Gustav Mahler first premiered his Symphony No. 8 in E-flat major, concertgoers were treated to a performance by more than a thousand orchestral musicians. Then, settle for an intimate gathering at a small, local bookshop that smells like instant coffee and charity shop cardigans.

This was so much harder than you thought it was going to be. Now, watch your loved ones' eyes glaze over as you casually discuss what you might like to do for your second book, as if this whole process hasn't been detrimental to almost all of your meaningful relationships.

APOLOGIES

All book acknowledgements are essentially apologies.

The author is basically saying, 'Thank you to these people for putting up with the intense amount of self-important bullshit I've been slinging in your general direction through the making of this book, and let's be honest, my entire life. I hope seeing your name written in the bit that no one ever reads makes it all worth it. Namaste.'

So here goes.

To Alison and Clive and the whole team at Penguin Random House, thank you from the bottom of the empty cavity where my heart should be for your superhuman levels of patience and professionalism as you held my hand through this mental breakdown in print. I appreciate it more than you'll ever know.

Mum and Dad, I'm sorry I've probably taken you for granted. I'm also sorry if I forgot to ask you about anything in this book. Please don't sue me. Thank you for your continued overzealous and at times misplaced support. I love youse so much.

Ceara, I'm sorry I don't reply to messages enough. I'm so lucky to have you. Thank you for taking me op-shopping, to the library and introducing me to the cultural touchstones that are now my entire personality.

Elia, Kat, Liz, Claire, Jorge, Max, Patrick and everyone who's in charge of my money. I would quite literally be dead without you. Or worse, I would have a job. Yucky. I think I should say here: I'm just never going to get better at replying to emails.

Wendy and Clive, thank you for having a second child. Really appreciate it. It's worked out quite well for me.

Luka, Alex and Hannah, thank you for being Dinner Club. It's one of the true joys in my life.

Joel, Jack, Daniel, Susie, Georgia, Alex, Gez, Cath, Zoë, Jinx, McLennan, Joel, McCartney, Sally, Paul, Greg, Zan, Geoffy, Ballard, Erin, Andy, Kelli, Nick, Lucia, Damien, Zillah, Nath, Cassie, Ronny, Hannah, Gemma, Iain, Ben, Kylie, Myf, Brian, Adam, Vic, Johanna, Katherine, Tom, Lisa, Pam, Aidan, Alyx, Micah, Nikki, Eli, Sam, Chris, Michael, Joseph, Laura, Eddy, Phil, Nish, Amy, Ed, Charli, James, Hannah, Joe, Amie, Michelle, Ru, Tom, Fenton, Thairin, Adrienne, Carmine, Nikita, Henry, Ed, Charlie, Steen, Claire, Chris, Sally, Mads, Andy, Bridget, Gideon, Susan, Tom, Ellie, Wes, Paul, Sune and heaps more. Let's have a lunch or something soon.

And finally, Kyran, I'm sorry about everything, and thank you for everything. What would you like for dinner?